Le Corbusier & The Architectur of Reinvention

Architectural Association

Architecture Landscape Urbanism 9
Le Corbusier & The Architecture of Reinvention
Authors: Tim Benton, Peter Carl, Hilde Heynen, Charles Jencks, Mohsen Mostafavi, Daniel Naegele, Fernando Pérez Oyarzun, Stanislaus von Moos

AA Publications are initiated by the Chairman of the Architectural Association, Mohsen Mostafavi. *Le Corbusier & The Architecture of Reinvention* documents the proceedings of a conference held at the Architectural Association in London on 10 March 2001. It has been edited, designed and produced by the AA Print Studio.

ISBN 1 902902 29 7

AA Publications, 36 Bedford Square, London WC1B 3ES
T. 020 7887 4021 E. publications@aaschool.ac.uk
www.aaschool.ac.uk/publications

Bidisha '04

Contents

Mohsen Mostafavi

The Architecture of Reinvention

Charles-Édouard Jeanneret set about the task of reinventing everything he touched, from himself to architecture. Famously, he began with his own name. His resonant pseudonym, Le Corbusier, meant 'crow-like', and he spent most of his career observing – as if from the air, like a crow – the wider horizon of worldwide developments in architecture, painting, writing, urbanism and politics. From this bird's-eye view he picked out the topics that interested him the most, before touching down to develop his work in more detail, through an interplay of the different disciplines.

Equally interesting, with regard to the range and diversity of his practices, is the way they were reformulated and represented, the way Le Corbusier controlled the reception of his work. Most architects, given the opportunity to publish a monograph, reproduce all the minutiae of their development, by including every one of their projects. Yet Le Corbusier defies such conventions. His eight-volume *Œuvre Complète*, for example, contains no buildings from the first 17 years of his architectural practice. By omitting these early works, Le Corbusier was able to present a stylistically more consistent body of work and – according to H. Allen Brooks, the scholar of his formative years – to 'promote the impression of a child prodigy'. Le Corbusier's skill in bringing together a wide range of important topics, and in manipulating their reception, is one of the main factors behind his spectacular success. In this, he is the twentieth-century architect *par excellence*.

In light of the systematic specialization and consequent intellectual fragmentation of contemporary architectural practice, Le Corbusier provides inspiration for alternative ways of working and framing current tendencies and trends. Even though he was an ardent proponent of Modernism, he had already recognized, by the end of the 1920s, the need to address the tension between the universal or global consideration of problems and their local circumstances. This is a topic which only now, over 70 years later, is receiving particular attention.

'Architecture', Le Corbusier wrote, 'is the result of the state of mind of its time. We are facing an event in contemporary thought; an international event, which we didn't realize ten years ago; the techniques, the problems raised, like the scientific means to solve them, are universal. Nevertheless, there will be no confusion of regions; for climatic, geographic, topographic conditions, currents of race and thousands of things still today unknown, will always guide solutions towards forms conditioned by them.' It is this notion of the range and the multiplicity of practices and their repercussions that forms the main focus of the essays in this collection.

This book documents the proceedings of a conference held at the Architectural Association in March 2001. One of the main catalysts for the original event was the publication of Charles Jencks's *Le Corbusier and the Continual Revolution in Architecture*, a text which also provided a point of reference for a few of the papers. Another recurrent reference is *Le Poème de l'Angle Droit*, which is one of Le Corbusier's most significant texts. The English translation of the poem and the accompanying lithographs have been reprinted here with the kind permission of the Fondation Le Corbusier. Many thanks are also due to Charles Jencks for his contribution and unwavering support, and to Katharina Borsi for her help in the preparation of the essays.

Le Corbusier, The Assembly, Chandigarh, 1955–61, enamelled ceremonial door.

Charles Jencks

they are not creative; they merely establish a balance. A matter of plasticity, pure and simple.

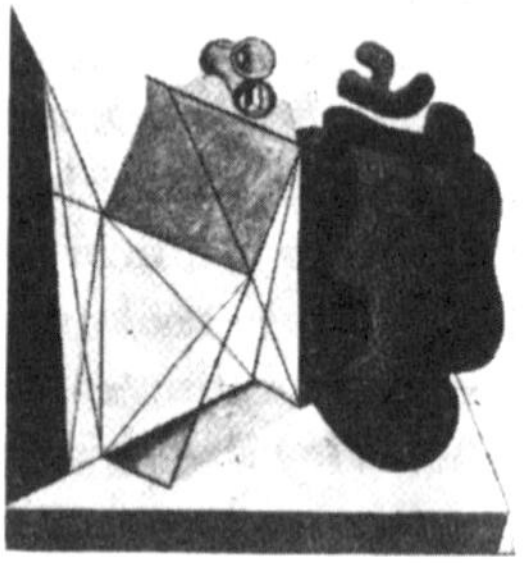

FIG. 4 A B C

Here are the façades of some houses and buildings designed at the same time as the paintings—small houses, public buildings, complex architectural groups:

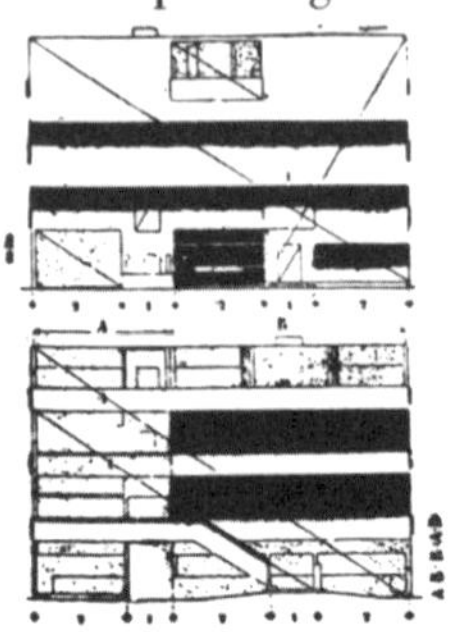

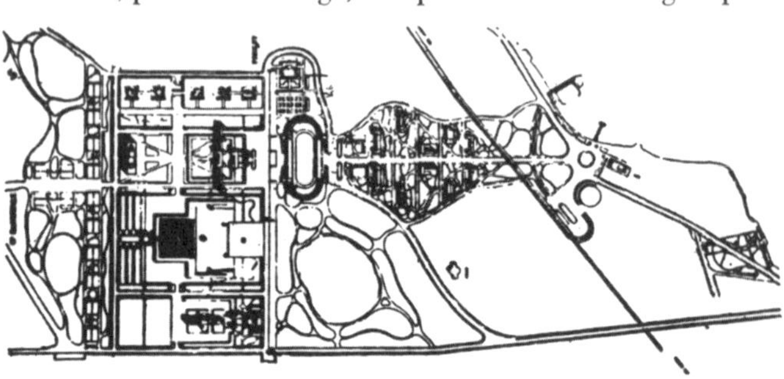

D E FIG. 5

Both the paintings and the architectural designs make use of the golden section, the 'place of the right angle', the height of 2·20 m. (man with arm upraised).

Le Corbusier and the Revenge of the Book

The revenge, of course, is on those who prophesied the death of the book. In the 1960s Marshall McLuhan predicted that print would become obsolete as electronic media swept through communication, but he spread the message through the book. And several of those he wrote are still in print. The obituary was in fact a birth certificate. The dreaded monographic tome has proliferated and grown ever bulkier, so that today Bernard Tschumi prints a fat silver book that weighs over three pounds, Norman Foster one that weighs over four pounds, and Rem Koolhaas one that weighs over five. This is progress: the weightier the message, the more profound.

Every architect today aspires to the condition of a fat book, Steven Holl small and fat, MVRDV big and fat. Why? This is a question that cries out for an answer and we find it first in our man from Switzerland.

Le Corbusier was the consummate architectural communicator, exercising his powers of persuasion not only through his lectures, which were performances of design on his feet, but also through his voluminous writing and illustration of books. He wrote some fifty-seven, and five times as many words as his closest competitor, Frank Lloyd Wright; indeed a thousand times more words than the average architect. On his passport of 1930, he did not style himself as a designer or painter, but as a 'man of letters'. The writing constituted a kind of challenge hurled at the world and, paradoxically, aimed at himself: it kept him honest to his architectural intentions and his mission impossible of changing the world. His adopted name, 'Le Corbusier', which sounds like a branded product – 'the architect' – was actually the accidental by-product of this writing, his *nom de plume*. So successful were his articles for *L'Esprit Nouveau* in the early 1920s that they instantly created a persona that swallowed his real identity – the so-far unsuccessful painter, the failed businessman, the unemployed architect. Having become embroiled in scandals with wealthy, provincial patrons, he ran away from Switzerland, away from La Chaux-de-Fonds and his former identity as Charles-Édouard Jeanneret. He took on this new character, The Corbusier, who he then christened in the third person as 'our man'.

Our man changed the world of architecture through his books. Anyone who reads his polemics – and they are still more widely read than

1. Page 35 from *The Modulor* (London, 1954), vol. 1: the contrast of various media – painting, architecture, planning – within the scope of Le Corbusier's 'universal' proportional system.

those of any other architect – will come under their spell. Even when one knows they are wrong-headed. Why? Because they use a panoply of rhetorical tactics in amusing, striking and creative ways, developing the inflated hyperbole of John Ruskin. Later, adopting techniques of multimedia presentation from the Cubists, Dadaists and his early associate Amédée Ozenfant, he fashioned a potent and mixed message. Its creativity often emerged out of the friction generated by juxtaposing one medium with another. A single page of *The Modulor*, for instance, contains three of his paintings, one building and one city plan – a typical opposition of different media and scales (fig. 1). These media informed each other and kept each other on the boil.

As if to underline this heterogeneity, Le Corbusier developed seven different writing genres – it is a number, incidentally, that crops up time and again in his work and one that some scholar will prove to have alchemical significance.

First were the opinionated travel journals, *à la* Ruskin, with their tart observations of architecture and everyday life. Second, and accompanying the above texts in later years, were the sketchbooks with cartoons, drawings and commentary – his thinking diagrams. Third were the architectural monographs, the famous horizontal black-and-white bibles known, in the manner of famous dead artists, as *Œuvres Complètes*. These were uncanny premonitions of things to come. They were written over thirty years, as if Le Corbusier could look back on his life before he had lived it and they are typically mixed genres in themselves. Their horizontal orientation/format may have stemmed from Le Corbusier's guess that, in spite of a thousand projects, he would produce mostly non-skyscrapers and therefore that ninety per cent of his photos could get full-page bleeds – almost a trademark of these publications. Certainly they are proportioned to the 35mm negative which is why every architect who got the message (such as James Stirling) followed the layout. The medium is the layout (fig. 2).

Fourth in his writing types were his four famous manifestos written between 1921 and 1925 and produced as monthly bulletins in *L'Esprit Nouveau: Vers une Architecture, Urbanisme, L'Art Décoratif d'Aujourd'hui*, and, with Ozenfant, *La Peinture Moderne*. In the 1930s the same type of articles, with the more horizontal layout of *Plans and Preludes*, led to the collection *La Ville Radieuse* (1935). All these manifestos compensated for their

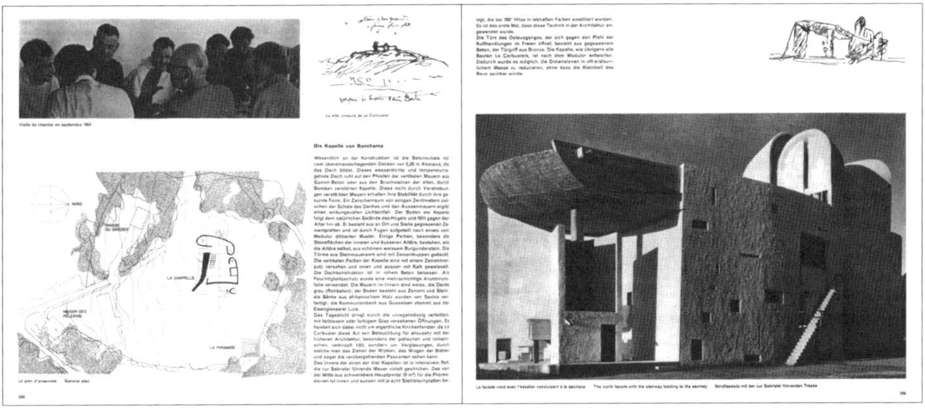

inherent zaniness (jumps in logic, sloppiness, photos stolen without acknowledgement) with a spontaneity and passion of argument, however specious it might have been.

The juxtaposition of stunning photographs made up for an ellipsis in thought and often constructed an argument more convincing than words could possibly have done.

In the 1930s, after his return from South America, Le Corbusier started producing the fifth type of writing, the lecture-sketchbook. These he created on his feet and later wrote down on board a boat or in a plane. Kenneth Clark used to say that turning lectures into books was the quickest form of literary suicide – that one could hear faintly, between the lines, 'next slide please' – but then Clark did not lecture with a pen and crayons. Le Corbusier 'performed' in this mode *Precisions* (1930); *Croisade ou le Crépuscule des Académies* (1932); *When the Cathedrals were White* (1937 in French and 1947 in English); *Manière de Penser l'Urbanisme* (1946), to mention only a few instances. He apologized repeatedly for their haste and awkwardness, saying they were part of the speeding spirit of the age and the difficulties of the profession, but perhaps he guessed his student audience would excuse the faults for the passion of expression and the bargain price. This was the time of pocket books with cheap line drawings.

Sixth were the poetic books and illustrated pamphlets, the more conventional picture-books with stunning photo-compositions by Lucien Hervé and others punctuated by captions, sketches and summary pronouncements. These could be on individual buildings, such as Ronchamp or the block in Marseilles, or on new technologies, such as *Aircraft* (1935), or on his own drawing and painting. The most explicitly poetic were

2. Pages 258–9 from the collected *Œuvre Complète, Le Corbusier 1910–65* (New York, 1967). Again the mixed media, but now in a didactic format with a description in three languages (French, German, English). The horizontal format was most suitable for the full-page bleed. The eight volumes of *Œuvres Complètes* became the most influential teaching books since Vignola (whom Le Corbusier purported to hate) and Palladio.

Poésie sur Alger (1950), *Von Poesie des Bauens* (1957) and *Le Poème de l'Angle Droit* (1955). The first of these contained his rejected city plans for Algiers; the last summarized his cosmic philosophy, in drawings, paintings and handwritten verse: 'dansant la Terre et le Soleil/ la danse des quatre saisons/ la danse de l'année/ la danse des jours de/ vingt-quatre heures/le sommet et le gouffre des/ solstices/ la plaine des equinoxes'.

The seventh genre was the mixed compilation, the collection of his whole life seen in retrospect: *My Work or Creation is a Patient Search* (1960) was the most convincing essay in this mode. Interviews and occasional articles supplemented this genre which was an exquisite corpse of everything – private and public life, self-advertisement, bitter complaint – and a brilliant demonstration of his message: creativity takes time and effort, but it lasts. Life is short, art is long and the book carries the message.

The Open Secret

Thinking and working in different media – enamelling, writing, painting, sculpting, city planning, drawing the bodies and faces of women he loved – was the spur to Le Corbusier's creativity and his self-reinvention every ten years. He often acknowledged the positive role of crossing media and particularly what he called the 'secret' of his painting and sculpture. These keys supposedly unlocked his architectural creativity. 'I think if one accords some significance to my architecture, it is to this secret labour that one should attribute its profundity'; 'It is there [in creating art] that you can find the source of my liberty of spirit, my disinterestedness, the independence, and the loyalty and integrity of my invention.' Because his work as an artist was often criticized and because he feared that clients and the public would not take seriously an architect who painted, he claimed that from 1923 his artistic activity was kept from the public view.

In fact he had regular exhibitions of his paintings (in 1936, 1938 and 1948), which he advertised through writings and books. Thus, by a strange immediate forgetfulness he produced Open Secrets, a genre which the public was urged to applaud and then instantly forget. There is no doubt this phantom limb helped him to transpose ideas, images and motifs from one medium to another and this transposition itself acted as a creative engine. Like the interaction of specialized areas of the brain, difference promoted creativity. This can be seen in his work on the chapel at Ronchamp and particularly in the plans (fig. 3).

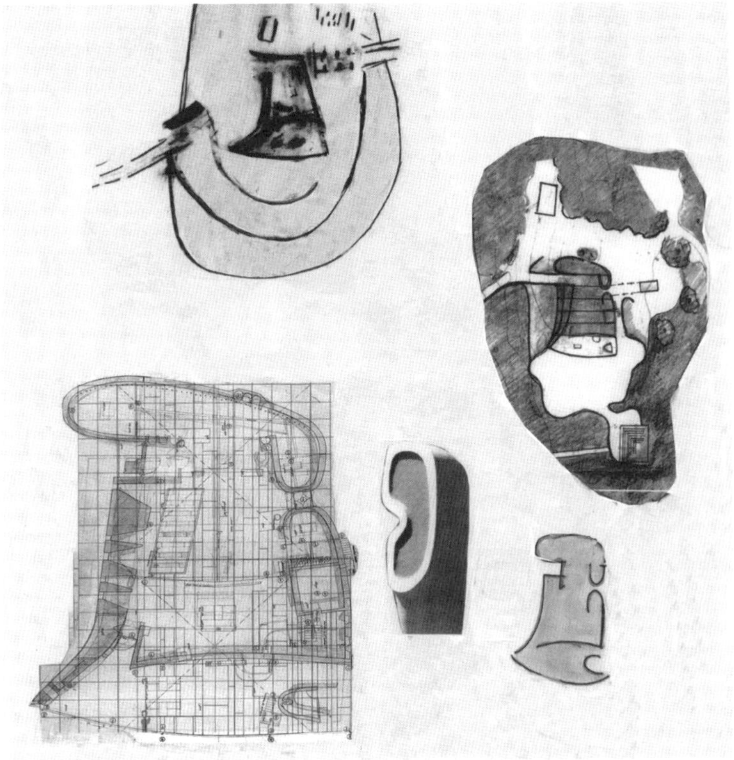

3. Analysis of Ronchamp drawings (all redrawn). Reading clockwise from top left:
a. Two main curves, the east with its altar and pulpit, answered by the counter-curve of an esplanade for 10,000 pilgrims and the bent, south wall drawn 6 June 1950 (FLC 7470);
b. Site plan showing Ronchamp forming outdoor space conceived as a cave or interior, (Maisonnier drawing, FLC 7481); c. Ronchamp as the character Ubu and a series of 11 fractal, self-similar curves (Sketchbook E18); d. 'Ear' or acoustic from sculpture of Ubu, *Ozon Opura*, 1947 (FLC 4); e. Ronchamp as distorted square. Two plans superimposed and edited showing conceptual grid and axes with the final lines in the floor and grid of windows (FLC 7455, 7169).

Here one finds themes brought over from painting and sculpture: his love for women, nature and visual metaphors such as the ear-motif. Acoustic parabolas, periscopes, curves in plan – eleven fractal curves – become the top calottes, ears as eyes that look over two horizons in the first drawing and over four in the others. Le Corbusier emphasized the mixed metaphor of synaesthesia by calling it 'visual acoustics' and he recalled an old image of his youth where the Parthenon also sent out 'waves and cries' that addressed the four cardinal points. But his plans and paintings reveal other concerns. The breasts, shoulders and buttocks of women he was painting are brought into the ear-motif, as well as the sign of infinity and the shotgun (fig. 4). He highlights other metaphors explicitly: the shell of a crab, a visit to Hadrian's Villa where the periscope motif was first drawn. Yet it is interesting that scholars and visitors – the initiated and the public – have seen still different metaphors. These vary from the prow and horn, derived from alchemy, to the nun's cowl and the ship, derived from popular imagery. Metaphors are 'a crossing over' and this is how Le Corbusier created: by crossing ideas from one medium to another.

Multiple Media = The Means for Creativity

The seven writing types I have mentioned interacted with the other media that engaged Le Corbusier – painting, drawing, sculpting (with Joseph Savina), etching, enamelling and photographing, as well as talking, lecturing and interviewing. My supposition is that these media or modes of discourse were, by virtue of their differences, a key to Le Corbusier's creativity. The media were not the message, but they did serve to give it precision, grace and inventiveness. How, in a turbulent century, was Le Corbusier able to reinvent himself at least five times? How was he able to become the Picasso (or Duchamp) of architecture? How was he able to: produce work in a regional Art Nouveau mode; then become a leader of the Modern Movement and International Style; then switch to primitive

4. Reading clockwise from top left: a. South prow of Ronchamp, also a horn and breast; b. The moon goddess in *La Femme et le Moineau* (tapestry detail), 1957 – her shoulder and left breast with its shadow become the prow; c. *Alma-Rio* (painting detail), 1949 – the pool/shadow doubles as arm, breast and part of buttocks; d. *Taureau 12* (painting detail), 1956 – buttocks and breast merge, are equated with bull's flared nostrils and placed above the silhouette of Ronchamp's prow; e. Sketch plan of Ronchamp, 1950–1, showing parallel between nostrils, buttocks and, to the right, f. The figure-8 of the waterspout, also termed a shotgun by Le Corbusier (collage redrawn).

SHADOW HORN
BECOMES BREAST AND ARM
shotgun
OO
infinity
SYNTHESIZED
nostrils
merge
B & B
infinity
Profile of Ronchamp
BREAST
ARMS AND
BUTTOCKS

materials and Brutalism; through Ronchamp and Chandigarh pre-empt Post-Modernism; and pre-empt High-Tech and Complexity Architecture through the Centre Le Corbusier and the Philips Pavilion? How? These transformations were helped along by the way one medium reacted to and commented on another. A work of architecture could be considered as a written text, a drawing, a model, a photograph, a sculpture, a painting or a detailed set of plans. Each medium challenged, clarified and refined it from different viewpoints. Each medium made use of different neurons, of different parts of his mind. The result? Continuous creation from different perspectives, a continual reinvention of architecture. The book was just one of the media through which these products travelled down a birth canal: they are, in that sense, a written architecture.

One can see in several of Le Corbusier's creations – the interior of the Swiss Pavilion, for instance, or the main door to the Assembly in Chandigarh – that the walls are covered in book pages. Sometimes images from them are even enamelled. Victor Hugo famously predicted that 'this will kill that': the novel and newspaper will kill architecture. But with Le Corbusier the book swallows the building – sweet revenge – or at least helps you read it (fig. 5). Architecture, like any ambiguous visual medium, is not finished until the captions are written, the comparisons made explicit. To drive the point home, he occasionally wrote them on the facade.

5. The front, and here back, of the enamel door on the General Assembly, Chandigarh, 1961 is a veritable text of previous book illustrations on Nature, Man, Cosmos and Number: the earth, the athletic Modulor man jumping hurdles, the pine cone, spiral, etc. The six-pointed blue area has been interpreted by Mogens Krustrup as an allegorical sign of Lake Geneva that Le Corbusier did not want to disturb – hence the cross-section of a building on pilotis next to it. The window-key sign opens pages on his books.

Daniel Nægele

The Image of the Body in the Œuvre of Le Corbusier

The house is a machine for living in.
Le Corbusier, 1923

To make architecture is to make a creature.
Le Corbusier, 1955

It is well known that Le Corbusier enjoyed reference and allusion.His early houses at La Chaux-de-Fonds alluded directly to the fir trees that grew beside them. His Salvation Army building, particularly in its upper storey as it meets the sky, assumes the profile of an ocean liner. In studies for projects in Rio, Montevideo, São Paulo and Algiers, his buildings are like bridges to be driven over; and by means both visual and verbal, Le Corbusier variously likened his Unité d'Habitation at Marseilles to an ocean liner, a filing cabinet and a wine rack. And perhaps most famously, he likened a house to a machine for living in.

'A dialectician, the greatest',[1] Le Corbusier thought in terms of simile, and in the late 1940s, when the devastation of war and the threat of nuclear destruction rendered technology a suspect platform for the promotion of modern architecture, these similes began to take on an archaic and subtly surreal character. Previously adamant about the virtues of precision and mathematical certainty, Le Corbusier began to ally architecture with art. His own painting served as a source of inspiration and innovation for his buildings, and in the mid-1930s it reached a turning point as he began to explore the theme of metamorphosis in a literal manner.

After the Second World War, Le Corbusier extended this exploration in his architecture. Like certain Surrealists, he began to conceive of – or, at least, to portray – both natural and man-made environments anthropomorphically. In so doing, he imbued his architecture with a dimension of spirituality and otherworldliness, veiling it in an aura almost extinguished in the mechanical age. Buildings metamorphosed into bodies and fused with the natural environment. These living works transcended style and internationalism to exist simultaneously in ancient, present and future time, and in the mythological space of the 'open cosmos'.

Did this go unnoticed? Perhaps it was sensed in the buildings, subliminally read in the carefully contrived images of the work. For how

1. Iconostase from *Le Poème de l'Angle Droit*, 1955, the key to assembling its lithographs.

in the mid-twentieth century to cloak a building in cult without rendering it kitsch? How to allow the curious, the polysensuous and the irrational to be born of the logical, the material, the functional, the structural? If these were the questions that confronted Le Corbusier as he moved to coalesce art and architecture, the answer for him lay largely in a single truth: the truth of illusion. For Le Corbusier, visual ambiguity accessed this truth. Cultivated for more than four decades in his many paintings, buildings and book illustrations, ambiguity provided the means to link the real with the ideal, the mundane with the profound. It served him as simile serves a poet; it was a discreet, covert manner of communication, while being the very essence of his art. Ambiguity allowed the figurative to be present yet hidden – accessible only to the privileged few who could see what others could not. The 'pictorial image of dialectics',[2] in the words of Walter Benjamin, it could portray the world as coded, laden with meaning. In Le Corbusier's hands, it made present the numinous.

What follows is on the one hand an exposé, on the other an excursion. It presents a case for the cryptic by taking the reader to sites comprised of highly ambiguous imagery – illusory representation carefully selected to reveal a truth. It asks the reader to adopt what Le Corbusier so often called for in his writings: a different way of seeing things. 'It is necessary to say what one sees,' he wrote in a passage that became the motto of several of his later illustrated books, 'but what is more essential and more beneficial, is to see what one sees'.[3]

I

The excursion begins with a subtle but climactic moment found in *Le Livre de Ronchamp*, the second of Le Corbusier's three books on Notre-Dame du Haut which serve as addenda to this famous pilgrimage chapel.[4] The book records the day of the chapel's dedication through a series of photographs arranged in a film-like sequence. In so doing, it cloaks the building in a narrative not customary to modern architecture. In image after image, the chapel is presented as it might have been experienced by the worshippers that day as they climbed the hill, ambled about the strange structure, noted its striking features, and ultimately penetrated its dark interior to be bathed in its special light. At the conclusion of the sequence

2. Le Corbusier's Ronchamp by night. A photograph by Hans Silvester from *Le Livre de Ronchamp*.

the reader is ushered outside where, at the chapel's exterior east altar, the formal dedication is underway. The day is over, darkness falls, and Le Corbusier concludes his story with a curious photograph of the chapel at night (fig. 2).

The photograph depicts a group of worshippers gathered around a fire just in front of the east facade. The figures appear as fragments, some as silhouettes, others as glowing faces and hands suspended in mid-air. Behind them the chapel emerges mysteriously from the surrounding blackness. It, too, is fragmented; and as the reader looks at it, a sense of the uncanny takes hold. For the firelight has transformed the chapel's facade into a glowing, benevolent face, floating in the darkness: curved balcony as nose, linear bench as mouth, the glass lozenge as right eye. Shadows cast by the fire reinforce this physiognomy and lend it a distinct personality by adding a bridge over the nose, a triangular lash above the eye, and a hairline where the wall meets the roof.

But what can be made of this 'appearance'? Fire to air, air to apparition – its 'make up' is like that of so many myths: the genie of Aladdin's lamp; Christian belief which equates the Church, Ecclesia, with Notre-Dame herself; the new spirit that resides in the body from the day of its christening. And yet there is something comical about this spectre that undermines any serious attempt to find allegory within its structure. If here we find a face at all, perhaps it should be accepted as little more than that – a finding which Le Corbusier found, and in which he saw an opportunity for a visual pun, entertaining yet hardly intended to be edifying.

Yet a cursory review of his writings on Ronchamp offers much evidence to the contrary, evidence that Le Corbusier, master of ambiguity, consciously designed the chapel facade as a face. A face is certainly present in all the maquettes and study sketches – even in the earliest conceptual sketch, which in addition to its Mona Lisa smile has a head of hair complete with stylish curly lock (fig. 4). This earliest face finds an ancestor in Le Corbusier's 1935 painting, *Femme Couchée, Cordage et Bateau à la Porte Ouverte*, where a skull-capped feminine figure with truly strange anatomy stares out with her right eye only, covering the left with her hand in a Last Judgement gesture (fig. 3).

3. Le Corbusier, *Femme Couchée, Cordage et Bateau à la Porte Ouverte*, oil on canvas, 1935 (detail).

4. Sketch of the east facade of Ronchamp, from Sketchbook D17, Summer 1950, no. 274.

The one-eyed aspect of the east facade is both its most disturbing and most distinguishing feature, and one that can only hinder easy acceptance of any suggestion of a physiognomy. Yet, many of Le Corbusier's paintings are populated with monocular female faces, usually hooded or 'hard-haired'. He sketched himself and his mother in such a manner; and in sculpture from the early 1950s – works contemporary to the refining of the design of Ronchamp – he gave the monocular face three-dimensional form.[5] Even in celestial bodies Le Corbusier discovered a one-eyed woman, recording in his sketchbook a monocular moon he spied in India, in November 1955,[6] a finding he presumably regarded as significant to Ronchamp, for the sketch he drew was later transcribed to a stained-glass window of the chapel and subsequently re-presented in photographs and drawings in his first book on this building.[7]

The one-eyed face, of course, was a staple of modern art, presumably because it allows both front and profile views to be presented simultaneously. Picasso used it as such, as did Brancusi, Chagall, Arp, Apollinaire, Léger and Redon.[8] Both Klee and Kandinsky used compositions that directly parallel the Ronchamp nightscene.[9] *L'Élan*, the journal run in the 1910s by Le Corbusier's Purist partner Amédée Ozenfant, was filled with one-eyed women, and Ozenfant closed his renowned *Foundations of Modern Art* with an aerial view of the pyramids, which anticipated by thirty years the Ronchamp countenance.[10]

The Ronchamp nightscene is also interesting for its bipartite composition. The image is clearly divided into two 'realms': the upper part where the glowing face floats, and the lower part where dark figures are gathered around the fire. Light and dark, sky and earth, heaven and hell, ideal and real – much can be assigned to such a duality. Many of Le Corbusier's compositions, including those found in photographs of his buildings, display this bipartite division, presumably to order them, but also, no doubt, because presentation in pairs – the creation of distinct and adjacent spatial realms – encourages dialectical thinking about even the most prosaic of subjects.[11] This disposition is particularly evident in the numerous lithographs that illustrate Le Corbusier's enigmatic *Le Poème de l'Angle Droit*, completed in 1955, the same year as Ronchamp (fig. 6).[12]

5. Le Corbusier, *La Main Ouverte*, watercolour, 1948.

6. Lithographs 25, 85 and 109 from *Le Poème de l'Angle Droit*, 1955.

25

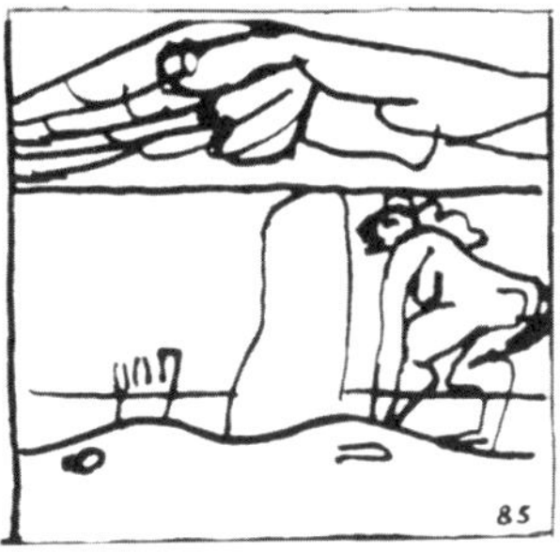
85

109

In each, an enormous, bizarre phenomenon floats in the upper half of the picture. The theme also found its way into contemporary drawings and paintings by Le Corbusier, such as *La Main Ouverte*, a watercolour from 1948. In the upper half, a colossal hand is suspended above a horizon line while below onlookers assemble (fig. 5).[13]

These parallel images encourage further interpretation of the Ronchamp nightscene as they present us not with simply a two-dimensional fleeting phenomenon, but with a kind of giantism. If the idea of a chapel with a face is accepted, it follows that the chapel itself is a head, an enormous head that sits atop the hill looking out towards the east. People can inhabit this head, dwell in its darkness, feel the light which penetrates it day after day. But from within, they cannot see out. Ronchamp: a head, a cranium, a colossal skull. The notion is fantastic and absurd, but there is much to recommend it.

II

Among the large collection of picture postcards in Le Corbusier's archive in Paris, is an image of a modest, partially ruined, stone building, the Chapelle Romane de Notre-Dame de Belvezet (fig. 7).[14] The facade is curious. Like the Ronchamp photograph it exhibits facial features. A mouth and two eyes, the right one considerably smaller than the left – perhaps winking – are the first clues. With a hairline of projected beams and an ear-like opening on its side elevation, the building is a compact, cubic head. On the back of the card Le Corbusier's inscription designates this tiny Roman chapel '*la naissance de l'architecture*': the birth of architecture.

Architecture is not built but born: it lives. Some forty years later, Le Corbusier interpreted his own creation similarly. On the cover of the small book Ronchamp he wrote that his chapel, raised from the rubble of a bombed church on a hilltop in eastern France, 'is born for today and for tomorrow'.[15] He dubbed it the 'Daughter of the Spirit, of which one knows neither from where it came nor to where it goes';[16] and by doing so emphasized its transcendent and phenomenal nature and underscored its fleeting yet persistent 'appearance'. Later, he gave a detailed account of the conception of Ronchamp. He told how, after having received the commission, he carried 'the idea of the chapel' in his head for several months. During this time he did not allow himself to make any sketches.

7. Chapelle Romane de Notre-Dame de Belvezet, postcard from Le Corbusier's collection.

'The human head is made in such a way as to possess a certain independence: it is a bottle into which one might place the elements of a problem, allowing them "to float", "to brew", "to ferment".'[17] In this metaphor the head is both box and womb. Once conceived, ideas gestate and take form. 'Then one day, a spontaneous initiative of the inner being, [...]; one takes a crayon [...] and scratches on the paper: the idea exits – the infant exits – it comes into the world, it is born.'[18]

The human head as a box in which elements float, brew and ferment: the description fits equally well a certain building type often proposed by Le Corbusier, the *boîte à miracles*. Though this box was never built, the pavilion that Le Corbusier built for the Philips Corporation at the 1958 Brussels World's Fair adopted aspects of its programme. Le Corbusier described the building as 'an Electronic Poem contained in a "bottle"... a stomach assimilating 500 listener–spectators, and evacuating them automatically at the end of each performance',[19] thus evoking flotation and fermentation while encouraging the notion of building as body fragment. In the darkness of its amorphic interior, visual and sonorous images appeared miraculously. An exclusively phenomenal architecture arose, composed only of light and sound in space. The environment was durational, the architectural analogue of ten minutes of the human mind.

This 'Electronic Poem', of course, was shortly preceded by *Le Poème de l'Angle Droit*. Composed of original writings and drawings, this publication was a curious hybrid of verbal and visual text in which the cursive, handwritten verbal took on visual form comparable to that of the line drawings which seem to flow from the same pen. Its twenty colour lithographs were designed to be assembled side by side to form a right-angled 'tree', a 'cross' which echoes medieval religious narrative art. The drawings often depict minotaur-like creatures: a woman-bull or a winged and horned beast metamorphosed from a human hand. Mirror-imaged figures – one white, one black, or one male, one female – are fused into unity. In both form and content the portfolio which transforms itself into a cross illustrates metamorphosis. It offers for consideration nothing less than a new worldview.

In *Le Poème de l'Angle Droit*, Le Corbusier placed his own creative energies in a cosmic context that transcends specific time and place. In its most revealing anecdote, he tells how he collected from the road a piece of dead wood and a pebble and how an ox passed all day before his window. 'Because I drew it and redrew it', he explained in the poem, 'the ox – pebble and root – became a bull.' Representation encouraged metamorphosis.

The mythic world that emerges from this metamorphosis is evident in the images of mirage-like visions, strange figures hovering above the horizon line as if the artist were depicting a seascape in which cloud formations were contorted into signs to be deciphered by the reader (fig. 5). The 'open hand' is one of these mirage-like compositions, a colossal body fragment that in the colour lithograph seems to float on a blue sea. 'Life is tasted through the kneading of hands,' Le Corbusier wrote in the adjacent text, 'eyesight resides in palpation'.[20] Le Corbusier proposed this hand as a centrepiece for his capital complex at Chandigarh, initially sketching it with several figures standing on its thumb, thus rendering it a colossal body part the size of a building.

Built as a rather large sculpture many years after Le Corbusier's death, the open hand monument easily falls within the acceptable limits of the modern architecture which, under Le Corbusier's direction, actively sought a synthesis of the arts. But seen as originally proposed – as architecture metamorphosed in the shape of a human hand skewered on a steel rod and left to wave in the breeze – the open hand is yet another affront to the canons of modern architecture.

III

A colossal head; a gigantic hand; a stomach or 'mind' large enough to accommodate 500? If such clearly representational, overtly symbolic and emotionally charged notions find no place within the context of modern architecture, to what realm do they belong? The *corps à habiter*, the body to live in, though antithetical to the logic of Modernism, falls easily within the sphere of French avant-garde art. For European Surrealists in the 1920s and 1930s, figurative colossality was a common strategy for enlarging art into habitable environment. Almost always, it was a fragment of the human corpus itself that was enlarged – typically the head, but sometimes the hand, the mouth, the genitals, the intestines.[21] Man Ray, André Masson and even Le Corbusier's revered Picasso paired man-made and natural environments with the human body, a fusion that resulted in a critical metamorphosis simultaneously poetical and psychologically probing. Such a fusion would have been attractive to Le Corbusier who, after all, had been trained in a Swiss Art Nouveau architecture that relied on nature as metaphor for buildings. After having entered the Parisian art world in 1918 as a painter, he had persistently aggrandized art into environments with pavilions such as L'Esprit Nouveau, Nestlé's, and Temps Nouveaux.[22] The idea of 'buildings as body parts' grew directly from this alignment of architecture with art, albeit with an art whose values, on the surface, differed greatly from those of Purism.

A brief history of Le Corbusier's engagement with such ideas must suffice to suggest a 'theory' behind such manifestations, a way of thinking about building not arrived at overnight, but cultivated over many years. It begins in the 1920s when representation itself encouraged speculation about the colossal. At that time, photographs and montages fragmented the human body into discrete parts which, through carefully conceived ambiguity, could be presented as enormous. This is most obvious in the work of Man Ray. His 1922 *Portrait of Jacques Rigaut*, for instance, shows Rigaut's head upside-down, isolated by focus and confronted with a tiny wooden *poupée*, the mere presence of which questions the scale of the head itself (fig. 8). Imaginary projects for 'body buildings' followed. In a 1936 self-portrait, for example, Man Ray graphically translated his own head into architecture by sporting six-pane windows as eyeglasses, and in his *Portrait of the Marquis de Sade* he described the high priest of Surrealism as a stone colossus comparable to the Great Sphinx. In his *Les Tours d'Eliane*, a fortress becomes female as towers and thighs coincide and building and body share a common entrance. In *La Plage*, this animation was extended to the scale of landscape as a natural land formation becomes a colossal reclining nude. Salvador Dalí provided numerous, more humorous variations on this theme, but it is the far more ominous images of André Masson that invoke the inherent power of the colossalized human corpus as architecture.[23] The head as a site for human habitation was from the 1920s a persistent theme in Masson's work and it blossomed in the late 1930s with works such as *City of the Skull* (1939) (fig. 9).

In Masson's projects, the body is depicted as an immense carcass without consciousness. The head is a helmet, and to inhabit it is for the viewer to assume the place and presumably the role of consciousness itself. In such works, the psyche is given palpable presence and a dialectic

8. Man Ray, *Portrait of Jacques Rigaut*, photograph, 1922.

9. André Masson, *City of the Skull*, 1939.

10. Le Corbusier, *Portrait dans un Paysage*, watercolour, 1908.

11. Photograph, probably by Pierre Jeanneret, of an apartment interior with a *poupée* on the table at the Immeuble à la Porte Molitor.

is established between body and being. A peculiar spatial realm is manifested. Colossal heads invert conventional scale, making the human experience Lilliputian and underscoring the relativity of the human perspective. Unreal scale does not replace but rather is placed next to human scale, creating a condition in which two apparently contradictory and mutually exclusive 'spatial realms' exist side by side.

These Surrealist paper projects were seldom realized, but when they were, as with the work of artist-architect Frederick Kiesler, they were contained within the realm of the museum or theatre as stage sets or exhibition sites in environments dedicated exclusively to fiction and fantasy. Such art projects suggest an elusive giantism of a similar, though less intentionally surreal, sort evident throughout America in the 1930s. There a new sense of the immense was present in skyscrapers, bridges, dams and ocean liners, as well as large-scale advertisements rendered in anthropomorphic and mechanomorphic form. The products of popular culture and particularly of the international expositions, these giants were intended for commercial and amusement purposes rather than for intellectual or artistic edification. In Tennessee, the TVA built an extensive network of dams to harness the forces of nature; while in South Dakota, Gutzon Borglum massaged a mountainside into the faces of four American presidents. Both projects contorted nature into a sign, imbuing it with an awesome and surreal mythic dimension.[24]

While both avant-garde and pop culture conceived of a new giantism, Modern Movement architects showed little if any interest in this tendency. Le Corbusier was the exception. His private files harboured overtly anthropomorphic images: 'le stand Ricard' publicity 'bar' at a 1939 Paris fair, complete with cartoonish roof metamorphosed into a face,[25] volcanoes photographed from above to resemble giant breasts and captioned 'Les deux "mamelles"';[26] Mount Rushmore under construction with Washington looking very much like Man Ray's *Marquis*.[27]

This interest in the anthropomorphic and the colossal was not new. As early as 1908 and again in 1917, Le Corbusier had depicted a kind of colossality in his watercolours[28] (fig. 10) and, as mentioned, his Purist partner Ozenfant frequently featured fictive colossals in drawings in *L'Élan*. When they co-edited *L'Esprit Nouveau*, the colossal emerged in photographic images of monuments and buildings and machines. The tendency is perhaps most evident in *Vers une Architecture*. This collection of essays first published in *L'Esprit Nouveau* and featuring a highly ambiguous illustrative text reveals Le Corbusier's pronounced tendency toward the physiognomic parti, an inclination also seen in works by Picabia, Suzanne Duchamp and Paul Strand in the 1910s.[29] More strangely though, in certain photographs of his architecture in the late 1920s, Le Corbusier employed wooden *poupées* in the manner of Man Ray, presumably to suggest a fantastic environment of competing scales (fig. 11). By the mid-1930s this tendency had grown more explicit, and in his 1935 *Aircraft* he complemented an obviously facial photograph of a fully-loaded aircraft carrier with the caption: 'And Neptune rises from the sea, crowned with strange garlands, the weapons of Mars.'[30] This association of ancient myth with the enormous realities of the twentieth century remained with Le Corbusier for decades.

In these examples Le Corbusier used the inherent illusion of two-dimensional representation to suggest both enormous scale and the aura of the human body in the new industrial landscape that he championed. In 1938 such suggestions were synthesized into concrete form with his monument to the socialist revolutionary Paul Vaillant-Couturier.[31] Expressly Surrealist, it featured a four-metre-high head placed directly on a shelf, mouth opened wide as if frozen in an act of speech. Hovering above it, an eight-metre-long hand emerged from a stone slab wall, presumably the sign of socialist solidarity. It had about it something both slightly sinister and highly emotive, something that bore little relationship to the rational and positive approach pursued by Le Corbusier in his earlier architecture.

At the same time, Le Corbusier – who had built almost nothing since 1933 and who would not complete a major work until 1946 – reintroduced himself as a painter with a major retrospective of his 'artistic production' in Zurich. For this exhibition, he issued a cursive theoretical treatise – ostensibly on painting, but applicable by extension to architecture – in which he stated clearly that he no longer understood painting as an 'objectification of a world' as he had in the Purist years. Painting had become for him 'an unlimited inquiry', an extremely personal and introspective investigation 'dans le monde apparent' which provoked 'a constant appreciation of the action of the objective on the subjective ... the transfer of exterior events into the interior of consciousness'.[32]

Thus, Le Corbusier silently moved from the absolute and material

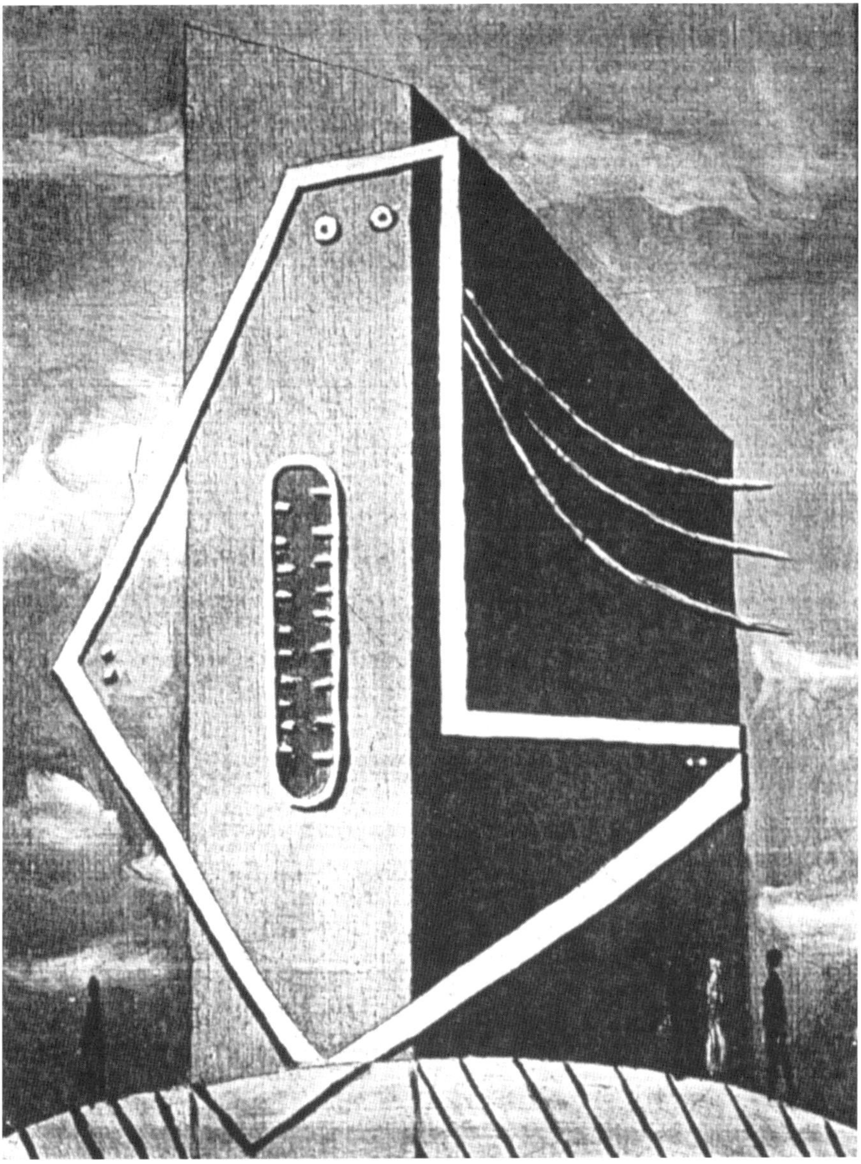

12. Pablo Picasso, *Monument (Woman's Head)*, oil on canvas, 1929.

13. Le Corbusier, drawing for chapel at Tremblay, 1929.

world of the rationalist to the relative and phenomenal world of the poet-artist; to the 'new world' of the twentieth century. Einstein, Freud, Breton, Leiris, Picasso – all could be accommodated in this new perspective. Ultimately it would lead to the proposal of a new 'absolute good' for architecture that Le Corbusier dubbed *l'espace indicible*: an inexplicable space that arose from the careful conjoining of the illusory space of representation – usually large-scale mural painting – with the 'real' space of architecture.[33] The colossal played a central role in that quest. It emphasized the relative nature of human perspective by providing a second perspective that questioned the authority of the first. It created a kind of visual contradiction that ruptured the seamless, ubiquitous space of perspective. In this sense it evoked a palpable space while at the same time serving as a means to imbue architecture with significance that it had lost in its quest for purity. With colossality, Le Corbusier shared common ground not only with the avant-garde artists of the day, but with the great builders of all ages. With it, he could transcend time and offer his architecture to worlds beyond his own.

IV

Perhaps Ronchamp can be understood as a manifestation of this transcendence. The ancient Greeks, some seventeenth-century landscape painters, and Surrealists in the 1930s would have seen it as such. So, too, would Picasso. In 1929 he painted *Monument (Woman's Head)* (fig. 12) whose geometry was remarkably similar to Le Corbusier's first church design, the 1929 chapel at Tremblay[34] (fig. 13); and in the late 1950s and 1960s he created actual colossi, totemic heads, such as the 20-foot-high concrete Ronchamp-twin *Femme aux Bras Écartés* (fig. 14) and the 84-foot-high *Head of a Woman* that effortlessly animates its oceanfront site.[35]

Of course, it is not certain that Le Corbusier intended the east facade of Ronchamp as a face, or that he conceived his masterpiece as a colossal and habitable head. What is certain, however, is that Le Corbusier was preoccupied with metamorphosis at this time and that transformation was at the very heart of his creative process. In ambiguity of representation, he found a means of transforming architecture – if only in the mind of the 'reader' – into mythic formation in which buildings could be converted into signs, and thereby access the cosmic order.

14. Pablo Picasso, *Femme aux Bras Écartés*, 1961.

NOTES

Parts of this essay appeared in my dissertation, 'Le Corbusier's Seeing Things: Ambiguity and Illusion in the Representation of Modern Architecture' (Philadelphia, University of Pennsylvania, 1996) and a longer, more detailed version was published in *Interstices* 5 (Auckland, New Zealand, 2000), pp. 36–53.

References to FLC (Fondation Le Corbusier, Paris) documents are to the boxes and numbers as categorized by that archive in 1993. The Fondation has since digitized much of its material and in so doing has changed nearly all of the reference numbers. No means of cross-referencing was established.

1. C. Rowe, *The Mathematics of the Ideal Villa and Other Essays* (Cambridge, MA, 1976), p. 194. This essay was first published as 'Dominican Monastery of La Tourette, Eveux-sur-Abresle, Lyon' in *Architectural Review* (June 1961), pp. 401–10.
2. Walter Benjamin, *Reflections; Essays, Aphorisms, Autobiographical Writings*, ed. Peter Demetz, trans. Edmund Jephcott (New York, 1986), p. 157.
3. 'Il faut toujours dire ce que l'on voit, surtout il faut toujours, ce qui est plus difficile, voir ce que l'on voit.' I am uncertain where and when this quotation first appears in the writings of Le Corbusier, but it is employed several times as an epigram introducing small *Forces Vives* monograms 'realized' by Jean Petit in the 1950s and 1960s.
4. Though *Le Livre de Ronchamp* (Paris, 1961) was 'realized' by Jean Petit, Le Corbusier wrote an unpublished addendum dated 27 June 1957 in which he explained that he himself was responsible for both the written and visual contents, including the *mise en page*; and that he offered this completed book design to Petit as a kind of gift to encourage him in his publishing efforts. It was published in 1957 as *Chapelle Notre-Dame du haut à Ronchamp* (Paris, 1957) and carried Le Corbusier's name on the cover.
5. For Le Corbusier's monocular self-portrait, see *Rencontre avec Le Corbusier* (Brussels, 1987), p. 48; for the drawing of his mother aged 91, dated 10 September 1957, see Le Corbusier, *Une Petite Maison*, p. 76; and for a one-eyed sculpture of a female figure, see, for instance, *Femme*, 1953, in Heidi Weber, *Le Corbusier – The Artist*.
6. *Le Corbusier, Sketchbooks, 1954–1957* (New York and Cambridge, MA, 1981), Sketchbook J38, no. 385. The text accompanying the sketch of the moon's one-eyed face reads: 'la lune le 26 nov 55 à 16 heures.' Two years earlier, on 26 May, 1953 at Chandigarh Le Corbusier had sketched the moon as a one-eyed female face and scribbled below it: 'c'est la première fois que je vois un visage à la lune'. See *Le Corbusier, Sketchbooks, 1950–1954* (New York and Cambridge, MA, 1981), Sketchbook G28, no. 944.
7. *Le Corbusier, Ronchamp* (Stuttgart, 1957). A photograph of the window appears on p. 18 and a sketch of the moon dated 22 April 1956 is shown on p. 24 opposite the opening page of Le Corbusier's written text, his 'Dédicace'. Above the sketch is written 'Autour du trentième parallèle nord, en Orient, la lune a un visage' and a bird in flight seems to emanate from the face of the moon. Both the moon, 'la lune', and the chapel, 'Fille de l'Esprit', are female.
8. The Surrealists' preoccupation with the single eye, epitomized by Georges Bataille's 1928 *Histoire de l'Œil*, is well known. It was stimulated by the work of Odilon Redon whose lithographs of the 1880s – *Il y eut peut-être une vision première essayée dans la fleur* (1883), *L'Œil comme un ballon bizarre se dirige vers l'infini* (1882), *Partout des prunelles flamboient* (1888), for example – are comparable to the Ronchamp night scene. On Redon, see Piero Falchetta, 'Anthology of Twentieth-Century Texts' in *The Arcimboldo Effect, Transformations of the Face from the Sixteenth to the Twentieth Century* (Milan, 1987), pp. 206–33.
9. Numerous works by both artists feature one-eyed faces. Both Kandinsky's 1930 *Upright* and Klee's 1931 *Landscapely-physiognomic*, for instance, could be read as immediate ancestors to the opening lithograph of *Le Poème de l'Angle Droit*, an image which Le Corbusier later recycled as a red-lipped lithograph and eventually as an enamelled wall panel for the Heidi Weber

Pavilion in Zurich. Klee and Kandinsky, both Bauhaus masters, were also understood by some French critics as fundamental to the Surrealist movement (see, for instance, *Cahiers d'Art* 7, 1928, p. 451). Klee's work especially was widely published throughout the 1920s and 1930s in the surrealist journals *Documents* and *Minotaure*. For *Upright*, see *Kandinsky Watercolors and Drawings*, ed. V. E. Barnett and Armin Zweite (Munich, 1992). For a very similar Klee composition, *Daringly Poised*, 1930, see Paul Klee, *The Thinking Eye*, p. 213.

10. See A. Ozenfant, *Foundations of Modern Art*, trans. John Rodker (New York, 1952), p. 315. If one were to protract this point, certainly the 1932 photograph, Viaduc d'Auteuil, by Le Corbusier's longtime friend Brassaï, would be included in this list. Its subtlety is such that were it not clearly framed in a photo essay in the magazine *Minotaure* – an essay in which all images anthropomorphize architecture – its visage might easily go unrecognized. See Brassaï 'Ce n'est pas trop tard,' *Minotaure* 7 (1936), p. 31.

11. For one of many examples of this, see the photograph of a Pessac unit captioned 'La terrasse' in Le Corbusier and Pierre Jeanneret, *Œuvre Complète 1910–1929*, p. 81 (upper right).

12. Le Corbusier, *Le Poème de l'Angle Droit* (Paris, 1955).

13. The Philips Pavilion 'spectacle' offered a three-dimensional manifestation of this *parti*. See, for instance the photographic projection of the reptile-like fon housed in the Musée de l'Homme, Paris as shown in *Le Corbusier, Creation is a Patient Search*, trans. James Palmes (New York, 1960), p. 281.

14. FLC, postcard, Box A1-8, no. 274. The card is probably from the 1910s, and the caption printed on the front of it reads: 'Villeneuve-lès-Avignon. – Chapelle Romane de Notre-Dame de Belvezet, dans l'Enceinte du Fort Saint-André'.

15. ...'est bien née pour aujourd'hui et pour demain.' This and the following three quotations are from Le Corbusier, *Textes et Dessins pour Ronchamp*, unpaginated (first page).

16. 'Fille de l'Esprit dont on ne sait ni d'où il vient ni où il va.'

17. 'La tête humaine est ainsi faite qu'elle possède une certaine indépendance: c'est une boîte dans laquelle on peut verser en vrac les éléments d'un problème. On laisse alors "flotter", "mijoter", "fermenter".'

18. 'Puis un jour, une initiative spontanée de l'être intérieur, le déclic, se produit; on prend un crayon[...] et on accouche sur le papier: l'idée sort, – l'enfant sort, il est venu au monde, il est né.'

19. Le Corbusier, *Creation*, op. cit. p. 186.

20. Translated by Kenneth Hylton in the unpaginated 1989 facsimile copy of *Le Poème de l'Angle Droit*. In French, 'La vie que l'on goûte par le pétrissement des mains/La vue qui est dans la palpation.'

21. Frederick Kiesler's work offers examples of most of these: for the mouth, his preliminary 1946 set design for Sartre's *No Exit*; for the genitals, his 1960–1 *Universal Theatre*, a colossal penis; for the intestines, his 1959 *Endless House*. See *Frederick Kiesler* (New York: Whitney Museum of Art, 1980).

22. For a protracted discussion of these three pavilions as 'art enlarged to the size of architecture', see D. Naegele, 'Le Corbusier and the Space of Photography: Photo-murals, Pavilions, and Multi-media Spectacles,' in *History of Photography* 22:2 (Summer, 1998), pp. 127–38.

23. Other variations on the theme would include Georges Malkine's 1928 *The Lady of Pique* and Roland Penrose's 1936 *The Invisible Isle*. All are featured in Patrick Waldberg, *Surrealism* (New York, 1966), figs. 89, 90, 139.

24. Although Gutzon Borglum's Mount Rushmore monument seems banal, this is contested in Simon Schama's account of the work in *Landscape and Memory* (New York, 1995), pp. 385–405. The surreal sense of the finished monument was used to great artistic effect in Alfred Hitchcock's 1958 film *North by Northwest* in which Cary Grant and Eva Marie Saint are confronted by the monument and ultimately traverse its faces as a means of escape.

25. See FLC Box C1–15, no. 54. News cutting from *Ce Soir*, 19 May 1939.

26. See FLC Box F2–12, no. 18. Page from *L'Illustration* without date or page number.

27. See FLC Box F2–12, no. 18. This news cutting is without source or date. It shows the Mount Rushmore monument under construction with a full frontal view of Jefferson and a profile of Washington.

28. For Le Corbusier's early watercolours, see Le Corbusier, *Peintre Avant Le Purisme* (La

Chaux-de-Fonds: Musée des Beaux-Arts de La Chaux-de-Fonds, 1987), especially p. 75, *Un Rêve*, 1917.

29. For an extensive discussion of the ambiguous photographic images of *Vers une Architecture*, see D. Naegele, 'Photographic Illusionism and the new world of space', *Le Corbusier – Painter and Architect* (Denmark, 1995), pp. 83–117.

30. Le Corbusier, *Aircraft* (London, 1935), fig. 18.

31. For a brief history of this project, see Jean Petit, *Le Corbusier, lui-même* (Geneva, 1970).

32. '[...]une enquête illimitée dans le monde apparent et une appréciation constante des réactions de l'objectif sur le subjectif: transposition, transfert des événements extérieurs dans l'intérieur de la conscience.' FLC Box U3-06, nos. 498–500, from a typed draft titled '"ŒUVRE PLASTIQUE" (Peintures et Dessins–Architecture) Editions Albert MORANCE.' A final version was published as the preface to *Le Corbusier, Œuvre Plastique, Peintures et Dessins, Architecture*, the catalogue for the 1938 exhibition at the Galerie Balaÿ et Carré in Paris. It was also published under the title 'Peinture' in 1938 in *Le Corbusier, Œuvre Plastique*, the eighth and final volume in Morancé's *L'Architecture Vivante* series on the work of Le Corbusier and Pierre Jeanneret. Annotated with sketches by Le Corbusier, this volume is devoted to the paintings and graphic works of Le Corbusier and also features the Pavillon des Temps Nouveaux.

33. For more on this subject, see D. Naegele, 'Le Corbusier and the Space of Photography: Photo-murals, Pavilions, and Multi-media Spectacles' in *History of Photography* 22:2 (Summer 1998), pp. 127–38.

34. In *Picasso: His Life and Work* (New York, 1962), pp. 240–1, Roland Penrose groups the *Monument, Woman's Head* painting together with Picasso's monument for Apollinaire and his later monumental sculpture for La Croisette, the seafront at Cannes. 'I have to paint them', Picasso told Kahnweiler in reference to such colossals, 'because nobody's ready to commission one from me.' This changed in the late 1950s. Le Corbusier's project for a chapel for Madame de Monzie at Tremblay – a kind of vertical Maison Citrohan made in the same year as the Mundaneum and the Villa Savoye – clearly anticipates in its severity the chapel at La Tourette. It was the starting point, the cubic ancestor, of Le Corbusier's more sculptural church of Saint-Pierre, designed for Firminy-Vert in the 1960s. See Le Corbusier and Pierre Jeanneret, *Œuvre Complète, 1957–1965*, ed. Willi Boesiger (Zurich, 1991), pp. 136–9.

35. For a listing of these outdoor sculptures, see Werner Spies, *Picasso Sculpture* (London, 1972), especially nos. 594–7 – four versions of the *Femme aux Bras Écartés* from 1961 – and no. 654, the 82-foot-high 1966 sculpture at Barcarès. For a detailed description and history of the sculpture, see Sally Fairweather, *Picasso's Concrete Sculptures* (New York, 1982), especially p. 48 on the *Femme Debout*, the 20-foot-high concrete version of *Femme aux Bras Écartés* built in 1962 by Carl Nesjar at Le Prieuré de Saint-Hilaire, Chalo-Saint-Mars, France. For a visual account of 'architecture-sized' Picasso sculpture, see the catalogue *Picasso in Chicago* (Chicago: Art Institute of Chicago, 1968).

Hilde Heynen

'Architecture or Revolution?' Le Corbusier and the Avant-Garde

The very title of Charles Jencks's *Le Corbusier and the Continual Revolution in Architecture* (New York, 2000) suggests that the author sees his subject in the light of perpetual renewal, as a man consistently able to take a new turn in his outlook on architecture. He might be considered the avant-garde architect *par excellence*, always ahead of the others, always marching in front. Yet that is perhaps too straightforward an interpretation. The meaning of the term 'avant-garde' has come to be understood in a number of different ways. Furthermore, since Peter Bürger published his *Theory of the Avant-Garde* in 1974, the socio-political connotations of the term have become of primary importance. And this complicates the applicability of such a term to the field of architecture.[1]

Theories of the Avant-Garde

Put simply, there are two distinct ways in which the avant-garde might be described. Both take into account the military origin of the term – a reference to the foremost section of a marching army, scouts that head into unknown territory. Since the nineteenth century the word has been used as a metaphor for progressive political and artistic movements that consider themselves to be ahead of their time. And it is in the different understandings of the relationship between the political and the artistic aspects of the avant-garde that the two interpretations of the term come about.

The more conventional interpretation does not overly stress the political significance of the avant-garde, rather it points to the avant-garde's readiness to fight artistic battles. Renato Poggioli's *The Theory of the Avant-Garde* characterizes the term via four moments: activism, antagonism, nihilism and agonism.[2]

The activist moment signified adventure and dynamism, an urge to action that is not necessarily linked to any positive goal. The antagonistic character of the avant-garde refers to its combativeness; the avant-garde is always struggling against something – against tradition, against the public or against the establishment. Activism and antagonism are often pursued in such a way that an avant-garde movement finally overtakes itself in a nihilistic quest, in an uninterrupted search for purity, that ends with a dissolution into nothingness. The avant-garde is indeed inclined

1. Le Corbusier, *Superposition*.

to sacrifice itself on the altar of progress – a characteristic that Poggioli labels agonistic.

Matei Calinescu also emphasizes the urge towards continual change and development as a typical trait of the avant-garde. According to him, the avant-garde's rejection of the old and its radical longing for the new drives it to a conscious quest for crisis, which provokes a term of continual revolution:

> Aesthetically the avant-garde attitude implies the bluntest rejection of such traditional ideas as those of order, intelligibility, and even success (...): art is supposed to become an experience – deliberately conducted – of failure and crisis. If crisis is not there, it must be created.[3]

More recently Peter Bürger's more politically charged interpretation of the avant-garde has assumed prominence. According to this author, rather than concentrating on purely aesthetic issues, the avant-garde in the visual arts and literature was concerned with the abolition of the autonomy of art as an institution.[4] Its goal was to put an end to the existence of art as something distinct from everyday life, of art, that is, as an autonomous domain that has no real impact on the social system.

> The avant-gardists proposed the sublation of art – sublation in the Hegelian sense of the term: art was not to be simply destroyed, but transferred to the praxis of life where it would be preserved, albeit in a changed form. (...) What distinguishes them (...) is the attempt to organize a new life praxis from a basis in art.[5]

The avant-garde, says Bürger, aims at a new life praxis, a praxis that is based on art and that constitutes an alternative for the existing order. No longer would society be organized on the basis of economic rationality and bourgeois convention, rather it would be founded on aesthetic sensibilities and the creative potential of individuals. Thus the avant-garde acts according to the principle of 'Art into Life!'

In the context of these trends of thought, one wonders how an understanding of Le Corbusier as an 'avant-garde' architect still holds. Does Le Corbusier, in his architect persona, indeed embody an avant-garde type, if one adopts Bürger's understanding of the concept 'avant-garde'? Is his continual revolution to be understood as the consistent implementation of purely artistic principles or has it also socio-political connotations related to the goal of 'Art into Life'? In order to answer these questions, this essay will address several elements that highlight different aspects of his work as related to the various understandings of the term 'avant-garde'.

Instances of Avant-Gardism in Le Corbusier's Work

As Jencks points out, Le Corbusier loved a good fight and saw himself as engaged in continuous struggle with the world around him. In terms of Poggioli's characterizing features of the avant-garde, it is clear that he shows the symptoms of antagonism as well as activism: he was continually seeking new areas in which to do battle, orienting his criticism towards the architects of the academy who failed to understand the spirit of the new epoch, towards the civil servants who did not take a favourable view of his plans, towards clients who did not reward his genius with appropriate fees, and towards former friends and allies with whom his relationships turned sour. There is also a sense of agonism in Le Corbusier's emphasis of the fact that, to his mind, he had given so much of his creative energy to the world free of charge, providing several cities with remarkable plans that – shamefully – were not appreciated by those who could have benefited from them. Le Corbusier can even be described as nihilist. In *Urbanisme* he recalls how an official denounced his plans with the argument 'you trace out straight lines, fill up the holes and level up the ground, and the result is nihilism'; he replied 'excuse me, but that, properly speaking, is just what our work should be'.[6]

In this way Le Corbusier is the embodiment of the modern artist: the heroic (male) individualist who lives purely for art's sake, renouncing the concerns of everyday life in order to devote his life to the higher aspirations of art, suffering hardships but firmly resisting all attempts to make him more pliable or conformist. As Whitney Chadwick notes, this conventional way of describing the life and work of the avant-garde artist often goes along with a positioning of women and women's bodies as a source of inspiration, as the origin of formal and stylistic innovations. The sexual and the artistic are fused in an equation that gives artistic creation equivalence with male sexual energy. Needless to say, in that same move women are presented as powerless and sexually subjugated.[7] This operation also occurs in the interpretations of the work of Le Corbusier, as is well exemplified in Jencks's book, which allocates a large amount of space to a discussion of the architect's relationships with women and what this implied for his paintings and architecture.

An important episode in this respect is Le Corbusier's encounter with two prostitutes in Algiers. The women were used as models for a sketch that during the following years emerged again and again as the basis for other drawings, paintings and ultimately even murals (fig. 1). Jencks's primary point with regard to this episode is to emphasize the productivity of Le Corbusier's fascination with these girls, with their bodies, and with their supposed sexual interest in one another, and the way in which he processed all of this in his subsequent creative explorations.[8] Some feminist scholars have looked less favourably upon this episode and its sequels. Zeynep Celik positions Le Corbusier's work in the long line of French colonialist endeavours to conquer the feminine heart of a foreign culture, drawing attention to several paintings and texts in which the city of Algiers, and especially the casbah, is presented as a female body to be conquered. 'Beginning in the 1930s', she states, 'Le Corbusier's gendering of Algiers extended this tradition to architecture. Provoking associations between the curved lines of his projects to modernize the city and the 'plasticity' of the bodies of Algerian women, Le Corbusier articulated his enchantment with these women and consistently represented the casbah as a veiled head in his reductive drawings'[9] (fig. 3).

Beatriz Colomina follows the reworkings of the drawing of the two women up to its final destination as a mural painting in E.1027, the house Eileen Gray built for herself and Jean Badovici (fig. 2). According to Colomina, Le Corbusier was trespassing when he did this mural, not simply because it was proof of his fetishistic desire towards these two women (that is after all only an individual and, some would say, rather harmless obsession), but more particularly because he executed the mural without Gray's knowing about it. Insult was added to injury when, in later accounts and presentations, Le Corbusier failed to mention that the house was authored by Gray, which has caused a longstanding misattribution in the literature.[10] With respect to the military logic implied

2. Le Corbusier, 3 *Women (Graffite à Cap Martin)*. Mural in Eileen Gray's house E.1027, Roquebrune-Cap Martin, 1938.

3. Le Corbusier, sketch of Algiers, with the casbah depicted as a veiled head.

Les Hauts
La Casba
le Bastion 15

in the origins of the term avant-garde, it could indeed be said that Le Corbusier acts out a role based upon exploring, conquering and colonizing new territories.

A second reason to see Le Corbusier as an avant-garde character, is his involvement with the avant-garde scene in Paris in the early 1920s, where he was part of the network that made up the intricate pattern of international relationships that determined the conditions for the development of modern art. *L'Esprit Nouveau* was, of course, an avant-garde magazine, taking its place alongside journals such as *Vesch/ Gegenstand/Object, MA* or *De Stijl*. Together with Ozenfant Le Corbusier also wrote a typical avant-garde manifesto, *Après le Cubisme* (1918), announcing the birth of a new '-ism' (Purism) as the latest fruit of the avant-garde tree. Yet within this act a certain paradoxical quality is recognizable. Purism claims to be the outcome of what might be described as a kind of Darwinist process of cultural evolution, leading towards a consequently pure and final result. Thus, while it is, on the one hand, part of the continuous cycle in which one avant-garde movement is superseded by the next, on the other hand it seems to bring this logic to an end, since it proposes a final condition in which all residual tensions are considered solved.

Third, Le Corbusier's well-known fascination with all things mechanical – cars, aeroplanes, trains, ocean liners, etc. – can be seen as a typically avant-garde interest (and is well documented by Stanislaus Von Moos and Beatriz Colomina).[11] Emphasizing the importance of mobility, dynamism, of all things modern, stressing the transitory and the ephemeral as major elements of modern experience indeed belongs, since Futurism, to the standard equipment of many avant-garde movements (fig. 4). Yet once again there is a curious bias that differentiates Le Corbusier's enthusiasm from the attitudes of other avant-garde groups. It resides in the fact that Le Corbusier seeks an actual cooperation between artists – or at least architects – and industry, an idea that is certainly not shared by all avant-garde movements. Indeed, movements such as Dadaism and Surrealism positioned themselves strongly against any compatibility between art and industry; Le Corbusier in his persona as entrepreneur (whether posed or real) sought a synthesis with capitalist forms of organization. This attitude was bound to horrify many other members of the artistic avant-garde, which predominantly perceived itself as anti-bourgeois and anti-establishment.

4. 'Maisons Voisins', from *L'Esprit Nouveau* 2, 1920.

Le Corbusier as Anti-Avant-Garde

There are two major arguments for positioning Le Corbusier outside the range of the avant-garde. The first has to do with his resistance to fashion, the second with his refusal to reconceptualize the field of architecture such that it coincided with building.

As to the first argument, one can trace a profound affinity between the phenomena of the avant-garde and fashion (both of which belong to the general category of the modern). Like fashion, the avant-garde reincarnates itself in a fast sequence of '-isms' inimical to their predecessors, which give rise to a reaction that overturns the prevailing mode, again and again. Jean Baudrillard has commented on this affinity:

> Modernity provokes on all levels an aesthetics of rupture, of individual creativity and of innovation which is everywhere marked by the sociological phenomenon of the avant-garde (...) and by the increasingly more outspoken destruction of traditional forms (...) Modernity is radicalized into momentous change, into a continuous travelling and thus its meaning is changing. (...) In the end, modernity purely and simply coincides with fashion, which at the same time means the end of modernity.[12]

Modernity, according to Baudrillard, establishes change and crisis as values, but these values increasingly lose their immediate relation to any progressive perspective. The result of this loss is that modernity begins to run away with itself and sets the scene for its own downfall. In the end the cycle of the avant-garde equals the cycle of fashion and this is as it were an almost structural feature of modernity.

With Le Corbusier, however, there is – as with Giedion – a very clear resistance to this idea of fashion. Mark Wigley has extensively analysed this resistance, claiming that modern architecture disciplines itself against fashion from the beginning. He quotes Le Corbusier, who states:

> As I believe profoundly in our age, I continue to analyse the elements which are determining its character, and do not confine myself to trying to make its exterior manifestations comprehensible. What I seek to fathom is its deeper, its constructive sense. Is not this the essence, the very purpose of architecture? Differences of style, the trivialities (*frivolités*) of passing fashion, which are only illusions or masquerades, do not concern me.[13]

In resisting the phenomenon of fashion, modern architects indeed take their leave from the logic of the avant-garde. As Giedion claimed in the 1930s, the roots of modern architecture have grown in conjunction with the avant-garde experiments during the first quarter of the century. By 1925, however, the desire for experimentation was over and the constructive stage of modern architecture had definitively begun.[14] Rather than favouring the 'tradition of the new' (an expression coined by Harold Rosenberg), Giedion accordingly turned to 'a new tradition' as the most adequate description of what modern architecture was all about – it is in the subtitle of *Space, Time and Architecture: The Growth of a New Tradition*. The difference between the expressions is a telling one: instead of glorifying the continual revolution suggested by 'the tradition of the new', 'a new tradition' suggests that there has been one last and final revolution, marking the beginning of a new order. There would be no need for further upheavals and crises.

Giedion's belief in the emergence of a new order is, to a large extent, shared by Le Corbusier. Although it cannot be denied that he regularly modified his outlook on architecture, he nevertheless had a kind of inner certainty that he had found some eternal truths of architecture. Indeed, for Le Corbusier, the answer to the chaos provoked by the era of mechanization lay in the eternal character of harmony and poetry:

> HARMONY is the important word for today. Put everything in harmony! Let harmony reign over all! To do this, let it break through, let it blaze forth, as a poetic phenomenon. Here is the collective enterprise! Poetry! The word needs to be proclaimed. Poetry which only exists in the context of associations. Associations which bring precise objects and precise concepts into context in a desired form.[15]

For Le Corbusier the new architecture harbours a close affinity with the classical qualities and eternal values embodied in ancient Greek architecture. It lies far away from the domain of fashion.

The most important argument in favour of positioning Le Corbusier within the anti-avant-garde, however, concerns the principle of 'Art into Life' that Peter Bürger sees as the most basic avant-garde credo. This principle was never subscribed to by Le Corbusier, who, although he was an enemy of the academy, was not after the abolition of architecture as an institution. Whereas he had serious objections to the way the academy taught the principles of architecture, he did agree with the separation it set forth between architecture as an art and building as a mere technical phenomenon. Indeed, Le Corbusier's theory is in many ways academic rather than anti-academic, since he continues to see architecture as founded on elementary composition (although in his hands this elementary composition takes on the guise of 'the masterly, correct and magnificent play of masses brought together in the light').[16]

Thus it seems that Le Corbusier's reaction against the academy never took on the same radicality as Marcel Duchamp's attacks on the institution of art, for example. Although there are some striking similarities between the gestures of Duchamp and Le Corbusier concerning specific works of plumbing, there is nevertheless a major difference in their approach (figs. 5 & 6). Both brought a common piece of bathroomware into an unexpected context: Duchamp by submitting a urinal – titled *Fountain by* R. *Mutt* – to an art exhibition (his only intervention being to put it upside down and to sign it), Le Corbusier by proposing to enrich the collection of museums with everyday objects such as the bidet. As Beatriz Colomina argues, Duchamp's gesture is clearly avant-garde, because it brings into question – and thus destabilizes – the very definition of art. For Le Corbusier, on the other hand, the distinction between a functional object and an art work continues to be valid and unquestioned. By presenting the industrial object in the context of the museum he does not insist on a change in its status; rather he pleads for an encompassing conception of the museum as an institution, so that it might become a more complete representation of an epoch. For Colomina, Le Corbusier is not acting as a member of the avant-garde here, because he does not make a move towards the abolition of art as an institution.[17]

Le Corbusier is at odds with some of his contemporaries, in that he did not question the status of architecture as distinct from the common concern of building. The early writing of Sigfried Giedion displays certain avant-gardist tendencies that Bürger would recognize. These take the form of an impulse which aimed at the 'sublation' of architecture. Indeed, in *Building in France* the author questions the very meaning of architecture:

5. Page from *L'Esprit Nouveau* 20, 1924.

6. Marcel Duchamp, *Fountain* by R. Mutt as published by Beatrice Wood in *The Blind Man* 2, a New York Dada journal, in 1917.

Maison Pirsoul

AUTRES ICONES
LES MUSÉES

Il y a les bons musées, puis les mauvais. Puis ceux qui ont pêle-mêle du bon et du mauvais. Mais le musée est une entité consacrée qui circonvient le jugement.

Fountain by R. Mutt

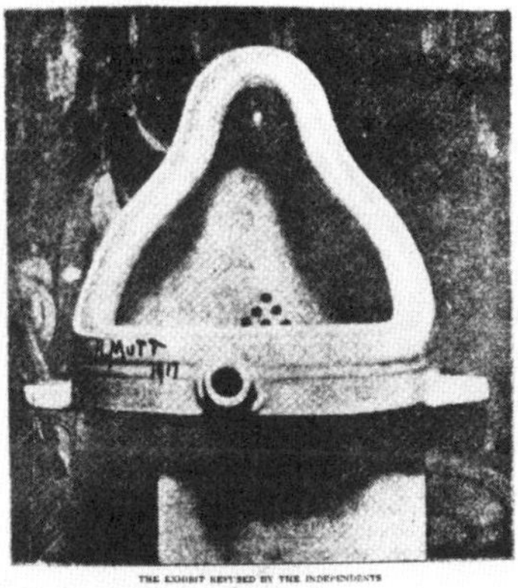

THE EXHIBIT REFUSED BY THE INDEPENDENTS

THE BLIND MAN

The Richard Mutt Case

They say any artist paying six dollars may exhibit.

Mr. Richard Mutt sent in a fountain. Without discussion this article disappeared and never was exhibited.

What were the grounds for refusing Mr. Mutt's fountain:—

1. *Some contended it was immoral, vulgar.*
2. *Others, it was plagiarism, a plain piece of plumbing.*

Now Mr. Mutt's fountain is not immoral, that is absurd, no more than a bath tub is immoral. It is a fixture that you see every day in plumbers' show windows.

Whether Mr. Mutt with his own hands made the fountain or not has no importance. He CHOSE it. He took an ordinary article of life, placed it so that its useful significance disappeared under the new title and point of view—created a new thought for that object.

As for plumbing, that is absurd. The only works of art America has given are her plumbing and her bridges.

"Buddha of the Bathroom"

I suppose monkeys hated to lose their tail. Necessary, useful and an ornament, monkey imagination could not stretch to a tailless existence (and frankly, do you see the biological beauty of our loss of them?), yet now that we are used to it, we get on pretty well without them. But evolution is not pleasing to the monkey race; "there is a death in every change" and we monkeys do not love death as we should. We are like those philosophers whom Dante placed in his Inferno with their heads set the wrong way on their shoulders. We walk forward looking backward, each with more of his predecessors' personality than his own. Our eyes are not ours.

The ideas that our ancestors have joined together let no man put asunder! In *La Dissociation des Idées*, Remy de Gourmont, quietly analytic, shows how sacred is the marriage of ideas. At least one charming thing about our human institution is that although a man marry he can never be *only* a husband. Besides being a money-making device and the *one* man that one woman can sleep with in legal purity without sin he may even be as well some other woman's very personification of her abstract idea. Sin, while to his employees he is nothing but their "Boss," to his children only their "Father," and to himself certainly something more complex.

But with objects and ideas it is different. Recently we have had a chance to observe their meticulous monogamy.

When the jurors of *The Society of Independent Artists* fairly rushed to remove the bit of sculpture called the *Fountain* sent in by Richard Mutt, because the object was irrevocably associated in their atavistic minds with a certain natural function of a secretive sort. Yet to any "innocent" eye

> It seems doubtful whether the limited concept of 'architecture' will indeed endure. We can hardly answer the question: What belongs to architecture? Where does it begin, where does it end? Fields overlap: walls no longer rigidly define streets. The street has been transformed into a stream of movement. Rail lines and trains, together with the railroad station, form a single whole.[18]

Giedion links the question of the autonomy of architecture as a discipline with the observation that the realities of space – streets, stations, etc. – no longer represent clearly defined entities; instead our experience of them is essentially defined by patterns of movement and interpenetrating elements. Giedion's implicit suggestion is that architecture no longer has anything to do with objects: if it is to survive at all it must become part of a broader domain in which spatial relations and ratios are of central importance.[19] Within this Giedion formulates a requirement that architecture break out of the limits imposed upon it by tradition and by its functioning as an institution.

Although he did not go on to develop these considerations in any radical way in his subsequent work, they were not simply examples of Giedion's idiosyncracy. His ideas could be said to have been shared by many prominent modern architects of the 1920s. As Sibyl Moholy-Nagy would later point out, the concept of the Bauhaus was founded upon the absolute unity between building and architecture.[20] The Bauhaus architects believed that their mission had to do with the design of all aspects of life and, consequently, they aimed at a reconceptualization of the entire process of building, from construction techniques and housing typologies to urbanism. Architects such as Walter Gropius, Hannes Meyer or Ernst May were convinced that their efforts should be oriented towards the whole of social reality. In keeping with this, they aimed at the transformation of the built environment on all scales.

It is doubtful that Le Corbusier shared these convictions. As Ciucci has pointed out, there were major differences in opinions and attitudes between what might be termed the French-speaking and German-speaking participants at the first CIAM congress at La Sarraz. These differences ran from social and political opinions to the conception of architecture and urbanism. For the German-speaking group, with Mart Stam, Hans Schmidt and Hannes Meyer as its most outspoken representatives, architecture and urbanism were but technical means to a social end: the reorganization of society according to collective principles. For them it was clearly understood that aesthetic considerations were of secondary value and had to yield to the primacy of more important general interests. Le Corbusier, on the other hand, understood this relationship as operating in reverse: transformation in architecture, according to him, did have to correspond to economic and social transformations, but this correspondence – far from turning aesthetics into a secondary value – resulted in a recognizable aesthetic idiom such as that of the five points (pilotis, *fenêtre en longueur*, free plan, free facade, roof garden). Whereas he was willing to acknowledge the importance of economic phenomena such as industrialization and standardization, he nevertheless did not accept 'definitions that would obscure the truth of architecture'.[21] For him the predominant objective of modern architecture had to do with architecture, and not so much with society. In terms of Bürger's conception of the avant-garde, Le Corbusier's ideas do not fit an architectural equivalent of the 'Art into Life' thesis.

Even where Le Corbusier's discourse hints at themes such as 'architecture or revolution', no real reconceptualization of architecture's role is at stake. It seems, therefore, that Walter Benjamin was wrong when he pointed to Le Corbusier as one of those who were anticipating the classless society in their architecture.

Transparency and Revolution

Walter Benjamin's ideas about modern architecture were very much influenced by Giedion's *Building in France*.[22] Benjamin, however, is more radical than Giedion in his interpretation of the social promises inherent in the new architecture. He recognized a Utopian aspect in the modern glass architecture, finding that its qualities of transparency and spatial interpenetration anticipated the new (classless) society:

> Giedion, Mendelsohn, Corbusier turned the abiding places of man into a transit area for every conceivable kind of energy and for electric currents and radio waves. The time that is coming will be dominated by transparency. Not just the rooms, but even the weeks, if we are to believe the Russians, who want to abolish Sunday and to replace it with movable days of leisure.[23]

The motive of transparency has clearly more than merely literal connotations for Benjamin. In this quotation he goes so far as to link transparency with flexibility in the structure of time. That time has become transparent amounts to writing on the wall for Benjamin. It is a feature of revolutionary moments that the linear course of time is interrupted. Thus, Benjamin sees the new architecture as an anticipation of a future social reality, one that will be characterized by emancipation and classlessness. For him, this is the promise of the architecture of the avant-garde.

This architecture was part of the avant-garde's attack on bourgeois culture. Just like Surrealism and Constructivism, it was preparing humankind for a new life to come. The new architecture trained inhabitants and users to adapt to new social conditions, which prefigured the future transparent society. Thus architecture was seen by Benjamin as a non-auratic discipline, capable of stimulating people so that they might align their attitudes alongside those required by the future society.[24]

Although, with this, Walter Benjamin suggested a very powerful and intriguing interpretation of modern architecture, it remains doubtful whether Le Corbusier's notions about architecture and revolution can be understood in this way. Indeed, the architect's own argument in *Vers une Architecture* points in the opposite direction. There, Le Corbusier's basic idea seems to be that modern architecture might prevent revolution. He corroborates this with three observations. First he states that the freedom provided by the eight-hour day necessitates another kind of dwelling:

> What is the man going to do with his freedom from 6am till 10 pm; from 2pm till night? What becomes of the family under these conditions? The lodging is there, you will say, to receive and welcome the human animal, and the worker is sufficiently cultivated to know how to make a healthy use of so many hours of liberty. But this is exactly what is not the case: the lodging is hideous and his mind not sufficiently educated to use all these hours of liberty. We may well say, then: Architecture or demoralization – demoralization and revolution.[25]

Secondly, he argues that a man who has the experience of the healthy, the useful and the productive in the factory or the office, will necessarily expect the same qualities of his dwelling. To this point these dwellings have failed to fulfil the basic needs of sun, of warmth, of pure air and clean floors. It follows, therefore, that there is a huge demand for the new architecture. Thirdly, Le Corbusier claims that the existing property arrangements are unfair and lead to a state of inertia:

> On the existing principles of property, it is impossible to establish a constructional programme which will hold together. And so the necessary building is not done. But if existing property arrangements were changed, and they are changing, it would be possible to build; there would be an enthusiasm for building, and we should avoid Revolution.[26]

His arguments are flawed in many respects. They are based upon a very one-dimensional, purely male perspective of the meaning of home; they rely on wishful thinking rather than on empirical data; and they are flawed in terms of logic, for the fundamental rearrangement of property principles he proposes would in all likelihood play out as a revolution. Indeed, this last chapter of *Vers une Architecture* is one of the weakest in terms of the logic of its argument (although the others are not much better – Le Corbusier convinces through rhetorical and visual means, rather than via the logical force of this argument).

It is clear from these passages that Le Corbusier was not primarily concerned about a classless society or about processes of emancipation. He was convinced that revolution should be avoided and that a massive application of his ideas about architecture and housing would be very helpful in this respect. Although he often paid lip-service to the interests of the common man, his first objective was to realize his architectural and urban plans. To do this he had to find clients, sponsors or politicians who would allow him to do so. His political views thus tended to be technocratic and reformist rather than radically progressive: an attitude that was to lead to an embarrassing alignment with the Vichy regime during the Second World War.[27]

Le Corbusier, I would argue, explored the reality of the first machine age from a very partial point of view, one that was in many respects conservative rather than avant-garde. This is particularly the case when he talks about families and dwelling practices, where it becomes painfully clear what a narrow vision he had. Although Walter Benjamin is willing to place Le Corbusier within the avant-garde of his time, this positioning is based upon a biased reading of his architecture through the more or less distorted lens of Giedion's *Building in France*.

As a result is it not surprising to learn that after the Second World

War the artistic avant-garde sought to distance itself from Le Corbusier. The most vehement criticism of him came from movements such as the Lettrists or the Situationist International, rather than from right-wing conservatives. Take, for example, the words directed towards Le Corbusier in the Lettrist journal *Potlatch*:

> In this epoch which becomes more and more characterized by oppression, there is a certain man who is especially repugnant. He builds cells as housing units, he builds a capital for the Nepalese, he builds vertical ghettos, morgues for a time which can use them very well...[28]

To the Lettrists, Le Corbusier exemplified a culture of technocratic oppression rather than one of liberating creativity. Insofar as he was ever a champion of the avant-garde, Le Corbusier was so in terms of the fighting and the colonizing implied by the military logic of the avant-garde. As far as its social commitment is concerned, Le Corbusier was not about to abolish the institution of architecture, nor give up an élitist position.

NOTES

1. P. Bürger, *Theory of the Avant-Garde* (Minneapolis, 1984). Originally published as *Theorie der Avant-Garde* (1974). For a first reaction as to the applicability of this term to architecture, see M. Müller, 'Architektur als ästhetische Form oder ästhetische Form als lebenspraktische Architektur?' in W. Martin Lüdke (ed.), *Theorie der Avantgarde. Antworten auf Peter Bürgers Bestimmung von Kunst und bürgerlicher Gesellschaft* (Frankfurt a.M., 1976), pp. 268–319.
2. R. Poggioli, *The Theory of the Avant-Garde* (London, 1982). Originally published as *Teoria dell'Arte d'Avanguardia* (1962).
3. M. Calinescu, *Five Faces of Modernity. Modernism, Avant-Garde, Decadence, Kitsch, Postmodernism* (Durham, 1987), p. 124.
4. Peter Bürger situates his interpretation of the avant-garde in the context of a historical evolution. According to him, the history of art in western society is characterized by an increasing autonomy of art as institution and system within society as a whole. The peak of this autonomy came in the nineteenth century with aestheticism, the tendency that extolled the idea of *l'art pour l'art*. Artists no longer saw themselves as artisans in the service of the rulers or as interpreting a higher ideal, such as religion; art was now pursued for its own sake. According to Bürger, the avant-garde was a reaction against this notion, for while art had become an autonomous institution, it had also became socially isolated.
5. P. Bürger, op. cit. p. 49.
6. Le Corbusier, *The City of Tomorrow* (London, 1977), p. 273. Originally published as *Urbanisme* (1924).
7. W. Chadwick, *Women, Art, and Society* (London, 1990), pp. 265–6.
8. C. Jencks, *Le Corbusier and the Continual Revolution in Architecture* (New York, 2000), pp. 200–2.
9. Z. Celik, 'Gendered Spaces in Colonial Algiers', in D. Agrest, P. Conway, L. Kane Weisman (eds.), *The Sex of Architecture* (New York, 1996), pp. 127–40.
10. B. Colomina, 'War on Architecture: E.1027',

in *Assemblage* 20, 1993, pp. 28–9.
11. S. von Moos (ed.), *L'Esprit Nouveau. Le Corbusier und die Industrie* 1920–1925 (Berlin, 1987); B. Colomina, *Privacy and Publicity. Modern Architecture as Mass Media* (Cambridge MA, 1994).
12. J. Baudrillard, 'Modernité' in *La Modernité ou l'Esprit du Temps*, from the Biennale de Paris, Section Architecture held in 1982 (Paris, 1982), pp. 28–31: 'La modernité va susciter à tous les niveaux une esthétique de rupture, de créativité individuelle, d'innovation partout marquée par le phénomène sociologique de l'avant-garde (...) et par la destruction toujours plus poussée des formes traditionelles (...) (...) A la limite, elle (la modernité) rejoint ici purement et simplement la mode, qui est en même temps la fin de la modernité.'
13. Le Corbusier quoted by Mark Wigley in *White Walls, Designer Dresses. The Fashioning of Modern Architecture*, (Cambridge MA, 1995), p. 38.
14. S. Giedion, 'Leben und Bauen' (originally written 1934), in *Wege in die Oeffentlichkeit, Aufsätze und unveröffentliche Schriften aus den Jahren* 1926–1956 (Zurich, 1987), pp. 118–21.
15. Le Corbusier, 'Le Corbusier replied:' in S. Giedion, *Architecture You and Me. The Diary of a Development* (Cambridge MA, 1958), p. 75.
16. Reyner Banham argues that there are many links between Le Corbusier and the theory of the Academy as put forward by, for example, Guadet. His analysis of *Vers une Architecture* is most relevant in this respect. See R. Banham, *Theory and Design in the First Machine Age* (London, 1960), pp. 220–46.
17. B. Colomina, 'Architecture et Publicité', in *Le Corbusier. Une Encyclopédie* (Paris: Centre Georges Pompidou, 1987), pp. 140–5.
18. S. Giedion, *Building in France, Building in Iron, Building in Ferroconcrete* (translation of *Bauen in Frankreich, Bauen in Eisen, Bauen in Eisenbeton*, 1928), (Santa Monica, 1995), p. 90.
19. As a consequence of this, the title of this paragraph should have been 'Architecture?', but the question mark was left out by the publisher – much to Giedion's annoyance. The correspondence on this subject is commented upon by Sokratis Georgiadis in the introduction to *Building in France*, p. 49 ff.
20. S. Moholy-Nagy, 'The Diaspora' in *Journal of the Society of Architectural Historians* 24:1, 1965, pp. 24–5.
21. G. Ciucci, 'The Invention of the Modern Movement', in K. Michael Hays (ed.), *Oppositions Reader: selected readings from a journal for ideas and criticism in architecture* 1973–1984 (New York, 1998), p. 563.
22. See the letter sent by Walter Benjamin to Sigfried Giedion, published by Sokratis Georgiadis in his introduction to *Building in France*, p. 53.
23. W. Benjamin, *Gesammelte Schriften 8* (Frankfurt a.M., 1997) pp. 196–7. German text: 'Denn in der Signatur dieser Zeitwende steht, dass dem Wohnen im alten Sinne, dem die Geborgenheit an erster Stelle stand, die Stunde geschlagen hat. Giedion, Mendelsohn, Corbusier machen dem Aufenthaltsort vom Menschen vor allem zum Durchgangsraum aller erdenklichen Kräfte und Wellen von Licht und Luft. Was kommt, steht im Zeichen der Transparenz: Nicht nur der Räume, sondern, wenn wir den Russen glauben, die jetzt die Abschaffung des Sonntags zugunsten von beweglichen Feierschichten vorhaben, sogar die Wochen.'
24. For a further elaboration of Walter Benjamin's ideas on modern architecture, see H. Heynen, *Architecture and Modernity: A Critique* (London, 1999), pp. 95–118.
25. Le Corbusier, *Towards a New Architecture* (translation of *Vers une Architecture*, 1923), (London, 1976), pp. 255–6.
26. Ibid. p. 261.
27. K. Frampton, *Le Corbusier*, (London, 2001), especially chapter 7, 'The Politics of the Unpolitical: Le Corbusier and the Saint-Simonian Technocracy 1923–1947', pp. 116–30.
28. Internationale Lettriste, 'Les gratte-ciels par la racine', *Potlatch* 5, 20 July 1954 (quoted from *Potlatch* 1954–1957 (Paris, 1985), p. 34): 'Dans cette époque de plus en plus placée, pour tous les domaines, sous la signe de la répression, il y a un homme particulièrement répugnant, nettement plus flic que moyenne. Il construit des cellules unités d'habitations, il construit une capitale pour les Népalais, il construit des ghettos à la verticale, des morgues pour un temps qui en a bien l'usage...'

Le Poème de l'Angle Droit

Le Corbusier

Translated by Kenneth Hylton, June 1989

A milieu
B esprit
C chair
D fusion
E Caractère
F offre
G outil

A.1 ENVIRONMENT

Men may
affirm this
beasts also
and the plants perhaps
And on this earth alone
which is ours
The sun master of our lives
far off indifferent
He is the visitor – an overlord
he enters our house.
In setting good evening he says
to this mossy earth (oh trees)
to these puddles everywhere
(oh seas) and to our lofty
wrinkles (Andes, Alps and
Himalayas). And the lamps
are lit up.
Punctual machine turning
since time immemorial
engenders every instant of the
twenty-four hours cycle the gradation
the nuance the imperceptible
almost providing
a rhythm. Yet brutally
he breaks it twice –
morning and evening. Continuity
is his but he
imposes an alternative –
night and day – these two phases
rule our destiny:
A sun rises
a sun sets
a sun rises anew

A.2 ENVIRONMENT

The level is fixed where
the waters stop flowing
to the sea
the sea daughter of droplets
and mother of vapours. And
the horizontal regulates the
capacity of liquid.
Solar rays powdery mists
condensation gaseous cloud
variable masses rising and
falling sliding over
each other rubbing up
against each other thrust
vertically horizontally.
Mobility has taken hold of the
amorphous
And from the Equator planetary
hot-water bottle clouds fly up
disperse, regroup
drawn in lines
meet and clash...
the storm bursts.
The heavens open water
has fallen it runs
collects it flows
and spreads

A.3 ENVIRONMENT

The universe of our eyes rests
upon a plain edged with horizon
Facing the sky
let us consider the inconceivable space
hitherto uncomprehended.
Repose supine sleep
– death
With our backs on the ground…
But I am standing straight!
since you are erect
you are also fit for action.
Erect on the terrestrial plain
of things knowable you
sign a pact of solidarity
with nature: this is the right angle
Vertical facing the sea
there you are on your feet.

Between bumps and in cracks
slipping on hard and sinking
in soft the crawling the
vermiculant the sinuant the
reptant have sketched the
first form of propulsion the worms
and snakes the worms hailing from
the potential of carrion.
The springs streams and
rivers do the same.
From a plane one sees them teeming
in families on the deltas and
estuaries of the Indus the
Magdalena or the margins of
California. Ideas too
grope their way tentative search in all
directions to the limit fix
the bounds to left and
right. They touch one bank
and then the other. Settle there?
Run aground! The truth is present
only in some spot where the current
always seeks out its bed! An
obstacle stands on the bank
will trigger the great cycle one
day begun. Meander will live
its adventure to its
absurd consequence moreover take
its time millennia
if necessary. The inextricable
bars the way the incredible! But
life must force a passage burst the dam
of vicissitude. It cuts through the
meander pierces the loops
sounding them out just where
licentious passage made them
meet. The current is straight
once again! And Savannah
and the virgin forests accumulate
countless stagnating
branches
The law of meander is
present in thought and
man's enterprise forms
renewed examples there
But the trajectory springs
from the mind is projected by
farsighted spirits beyond
confusion

A.5 ENVIRONMENT

Between poles reigns the tension
of fluids the scores
of opposites are settled an
end to the hatred of
irreconcilables is
proposed union ripens
the fruit of confrontation
The current pushes through and resolves
has pushed through and resolved.
I thought two hands
and their fingers entwined
might express the left and
right pitiless standing together
and so necessarily
be reconciled
Sole possibility of survival
that life has to offer

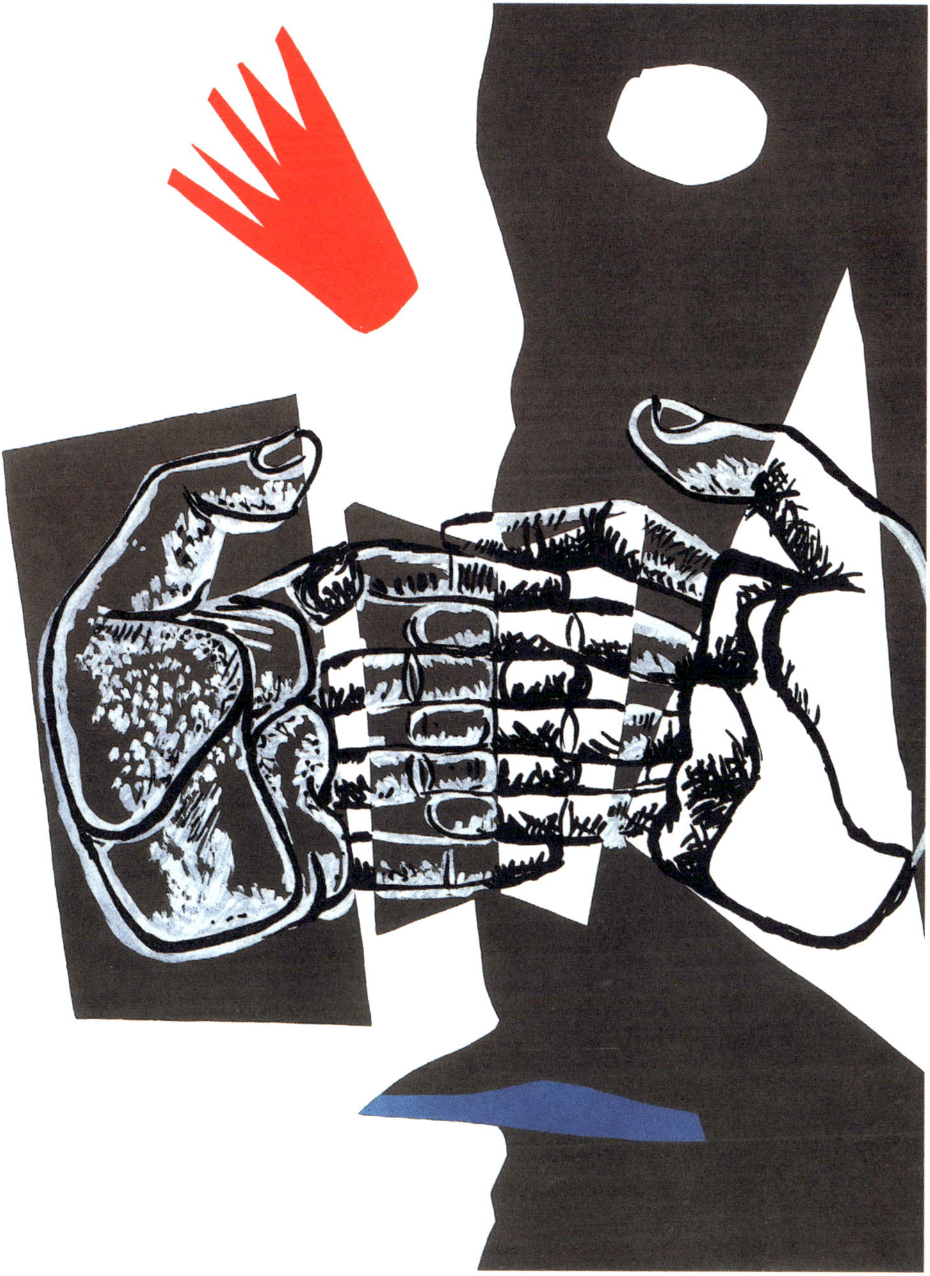

B.2 MIND

To place at the tips of one's fingers
above all in one's head an
agile instrument capable of swelling
the harvest of invention
clearing the path of thorns
clearing the way will confer
freedom on your freedom.
Spark stolen from the flame
the Gods nourished to
make the world play...
Mathematics!
Here is a fact: the fortunate
miraculous meeting perhaps of one
among several numbers has
furnished men with this tool.
Appreciative the philosopher
said, "Good shall be simple
and evil difficult"
Its value resides
in this: the human body
has chosen number as its
admissible vehicle.
... Whence proportion
proportion which orders
the relations with our
surroundings.

Why not?
What matter
the opinion of
the whale, the
rock eagle or the bee
in this context.

B.3 MIND

Freer of fetters than
before the house of
man mistress of his forms
takes its place within nature
Whole in itself
coming to terms with the terrain
open to the four horizons
lends its roof
to the company of clouds
of azure or the stars
Informed watch the owl
has found its own way
here
without being called.

B.4 MIND

Just as the negroes of Harlem
are united by exactitude
not touching but
at distances that
vary every second
In the same way
the Earth and Sun dance
the dance of four seasons
the dance of the year
the dance of the
twenty-four hour day
the summit and chasm of
solstice
the plain of equinox
The solar clock and calendar have given
architecture the 'sun-breaker'
placed before the glass surfaces
of modern buildings. An
architectural symphony
composed with this title:
'The house, daughter of the sun'
... And Vignola – at last – has had his chips!
Thank you!
Victory!

C.I FLESH

Armed with devices inspired with
precautions to pinpoint
seize stave in taste all
senses alert this is the hunt
armed to the teeth
muzzle nostril eye and
horn hair standing on end
and off to war
Beelzebub
Who is Beelzebub
in fact?

The elements of vision are summoned
together. The key is a
stump of dead wood and a pebble
both picked up in a
sunken Pyrenean lane. Ox
and plough passed
all day before my window.
Because I drew it and redrew it
the ox – pebble and root –
became a bull.
And to equip its force with scent
here is a dog, alert.
Thus eight years on
the memory took shape of "Brush"
(the name I gave to my dog)
he turned bad
without knowing and I had to
kill him.

C.2 FLESH

Woman always somewhere
at crossroads proves
that love is a question of fate
of number and chance
where the accidental even
inexorable meeting of two
roads is suddenly marked
with amazing joy.
One can be two and being two
be unable to conjugate things
it is essential to
bring together each
alas quite blind not
seeing the ineffable something
which he holds at arm's length. Inert!
Countless sleep in this way
but others know how to
open an eye.
For home from home is
in the great cavern of
sleep that other side of
life at night. How
rich alive is night in the
warehouses collections
libraries museums of
sleep! A woman passes.
Oh! I was sleeping, forgive me!
In the hope of seizing
my chance I held out my hand
Love is a word without
frontiers. It is also it is moreover
a human invention an attempt
an adventure.

Tenderness!
Seashell the Sea in us has never
ceased to wash its wrecks of
laughing harmony upon the shore.
Hand kneading hand caressing
hand brushing. The hand and the
seashell love each other.

———

In what we are speaking of here
an absolute sublime accomplishment
intervenes it is the harmony
of tense the penetration of
forms proportion – the ineffable
in the end precludes
the control
of
reason
carried beyond
all
diurnal
reality
admitted
to the heart
of an
illumination
God
incarnate
in
the illusion
the perception
of truth
perhaps
indeed

———

———

Yet one
must be
down to
earth alert
to
attend
one's own
wedding
to be
at home
with one's bag of bones
to go about one's business
and give thanks to the Creator

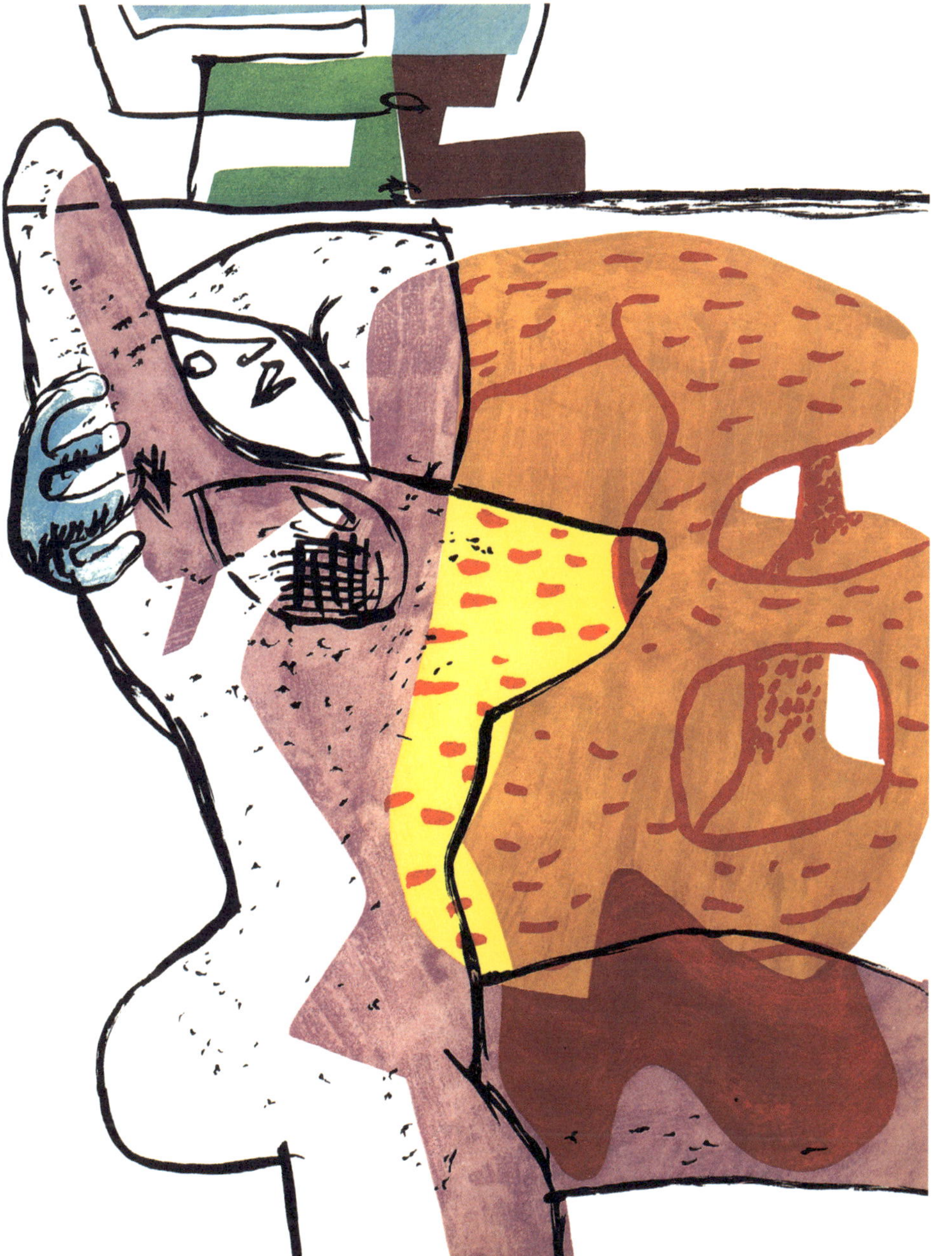

C.4 FLESH

Men tell of
woman in their poems
and music
Their sides eternally rent
from top to
bottom. They are but
half, and feed
life but by half
And the second half comes
to them and binds
And good or evil come
to all those
who encounter each other!

C.5 FLESH

The vessel drifts on
with songs on board
How all becomes strange
and is changed
carried up
and reflected at
the level of elation

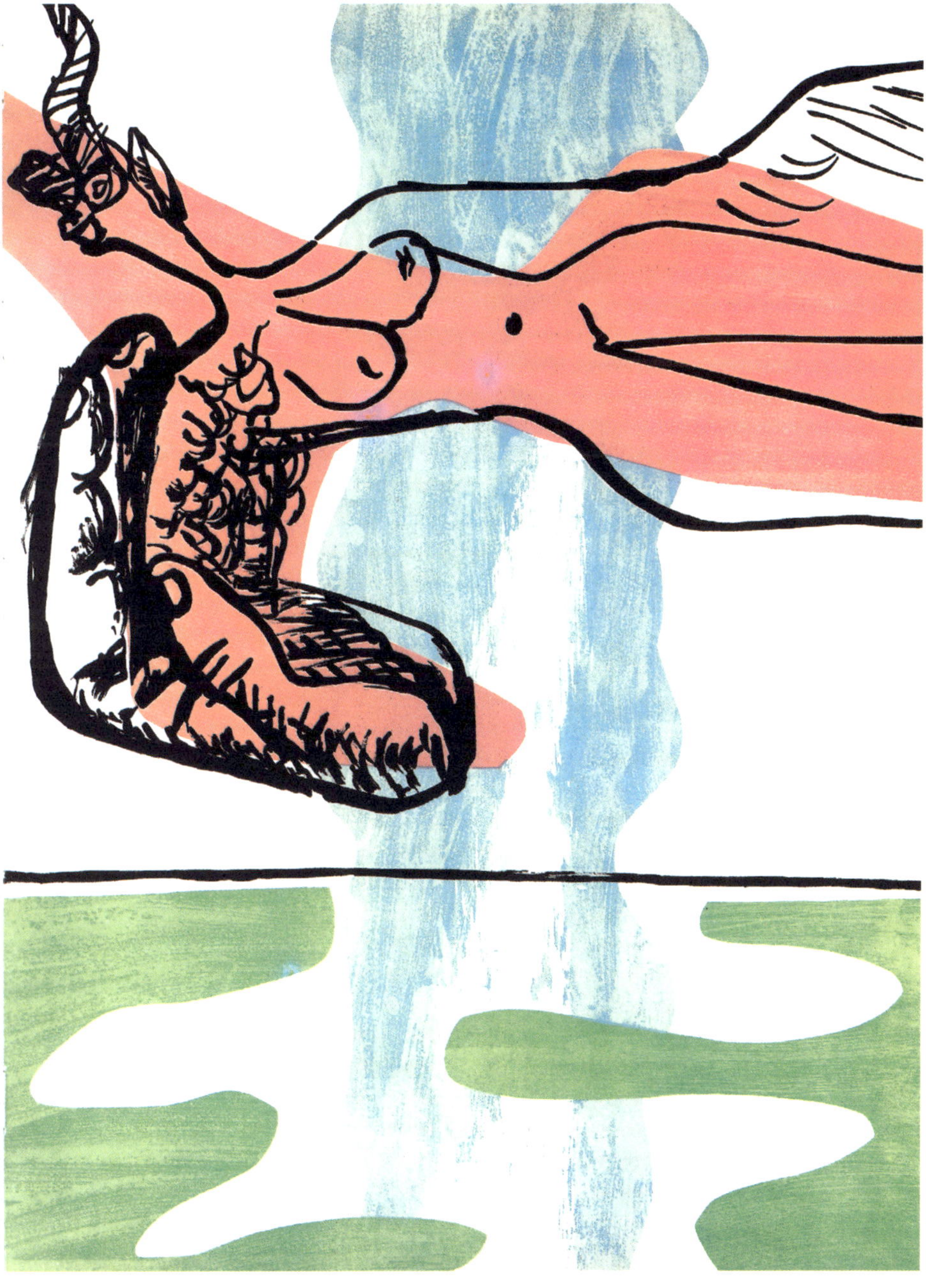

D.3 FUSION

Mistaking too many mediate causes
mistaking our lives
and the others are there
and everywhere we hear "No!"
And always fewer for
than against
Thus do not condemn those
who wish to take their share of
risks in life. Tolerate
the fusion of metals
the alchemies in
any case commit you
to nothing
It is through the doors of
open eyes that looks
exchanged have led to
the flash of communion
"The blossoming great
silences..."
The sea has gone out the
tide at low ebb will
rise again in time
A new time has begun
a phase a limit a transition
And thus we shall not
have mistaken our lives.

E.2 CHARACTERS

A fish – crossings
(and vexations)
A horse – campaigns
(and battles)
the Amazons ready
Depart go return and
depart again and
fight struggle always
soldier
Amazons are youthful
do not age.

E.3 CHARACTERS

Categorical
right angle of character
the heart's spirit.
I gazed in the mirror of character
and found myself there
found in me
found
Looking ahead horizontal,
arrows
She is right she rules
and knows height
does not know it
Who made her thus where does she
come from?
She is rightness child of
limpid heart present on earth
close to me. Daily acts of
humility vouch for
her greatness.

E.4 CHARACTERS

I am a builder
of houses and of palaces
I live among men
amid their tangled web
of being.
To make architecture is
to make a creature. To be
full to fill oneself to have filled
oneself to burst exult
icy cold amid the
complexities become a happy
young dog.
Become order.
The modern cathedrals
will be built upon this
alignment of fish
of horses of Amazons
constancy rightness
patience waiting desire
and vigilance.
Will emerge I can feel it
the splendour of raw concrete
and the greatness that was
essential to imagine the marriage
of lines
weighing up the forms
Weighing up…

F.3 OFFERING (THE OPEN HAND)

It is open because
all is present available
knowable
Open to receive
Open also that others
might come and take
The waters flow
the sun provides light
Complexities have woven
their fabric
the fluids are everywhere.
Tools in the hand
Caresses from the hand
Life is tasted through
the kneading of hands
eyesight resides in
palpatation

Full hand I received
full hand I now give

G.3 INSTRUMENT

With carbon
we have
traced the right angle
the sign
It is the answer and the guide
the fact
an answer
a choice
It is simple and naked
yet knowable
The savants will talk
of relativity and rigour
But conscience
makes it a sign
It is the answer and the guide
the fact
my answer
my choice.

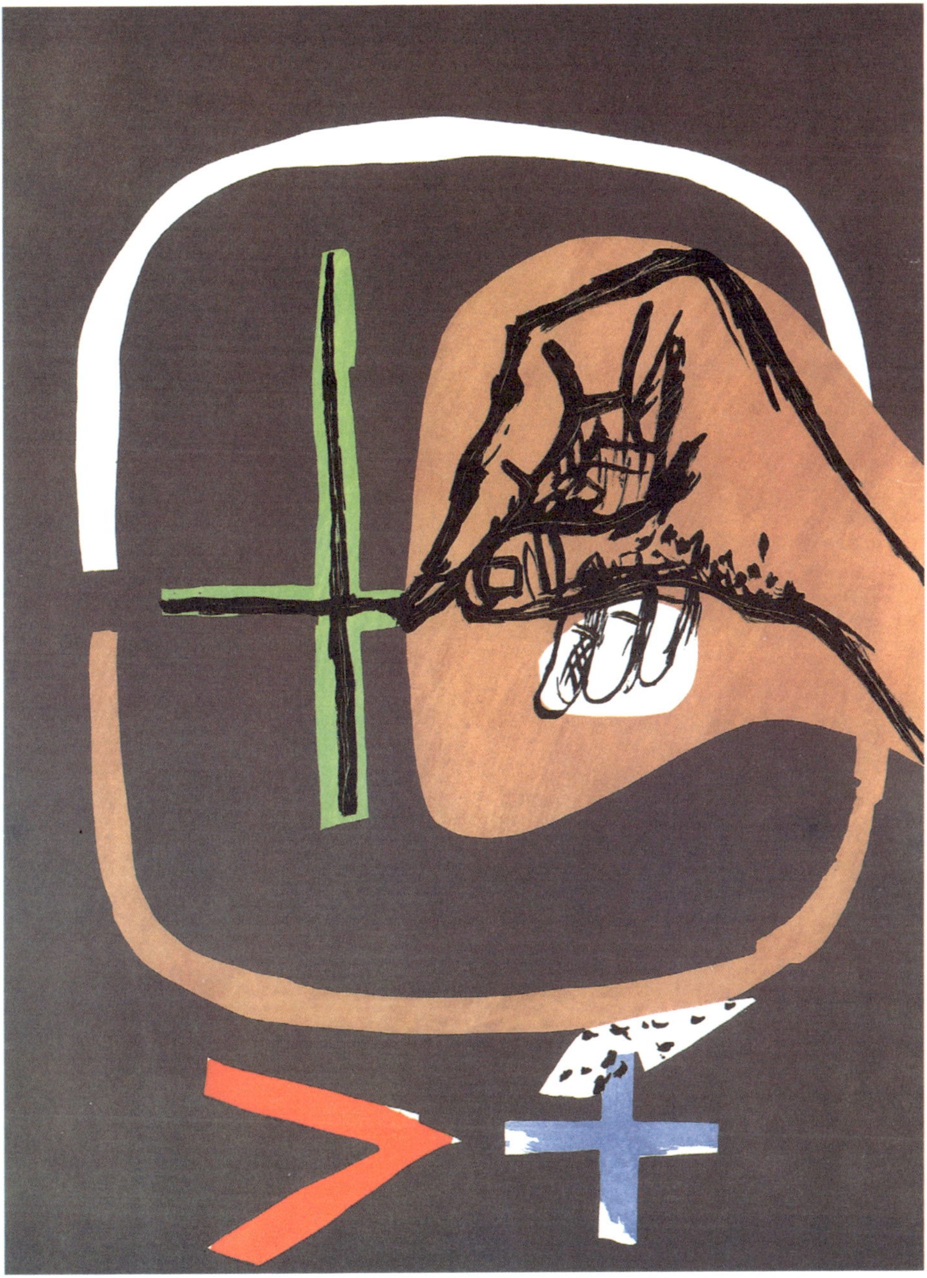

Peter Carl

The Tower of Shadows

To the usual interpretations of Le Corbusier's work in terms of 'form and space' has recently been added iconography, which finds personal themes, alchemy and primitivist elements of what is termed his 'cosmology'. The exchange between form and iconography rehearses that between Composition and Style of the École des Beaux-Arts, and places architecture at the disposal of conceptual styles of thought. As a matter of Corbusian interpretation, it also subjects the 'cosmos' to the private determination of the designer and to the particular buildings where this unique cosmos might be found.

The freedom to operate in this fashion is granted by the museum culture which allows one to confect a 'reality' from more or less arbitrarily selected fragments. In conformity with a general overestimation of our powers of representation, we find ourselves in an economy where the highest themes can be obtained on credit, through the exercise of 'reference'. If 'space' is the receptacle of all these references, and therefore of this conception of 'cosmos', is architecture subsumed within the referential structure? This question arises in the interpretation of the late works of Le Corbusier, which are seen to represent a spectrum from primitivist embodiment (the chapel at Ronchamp) to pure manipulation of images (Philips Pavilion), with the three-dimensional large-scale collage – that persistent ideal of Modernism – providing the means of exchange between them.

This view is partially accurate, and will be the natural result of anyone deriving the architecture from the painting and writings. These are the domains in which the iconography is most explicit, whereas his architecture is consistently more laconic. There is evident in his work a stratification of representations – from architecture through paintings to the writings – whereby the first provides the conditions for the second, and so on. The present essay seeks to clarify this fundamental role

1. Tower of Shadows, plan reconstruction – composite plan derived from atelier drawings (two drawings having the same number: FLC 29125). The cupola is superimposed upon the ground (esplanade level) plan, and both are set into the site plan. The cupola shows a complex – or awkward – difference of rhythm in each face, the four brise-soleil of the northeast face accounting for the distortion of the inner rhomboid. In grey is the undercutting (FLC 5809) of the Pit of Consideration with, in white, two of the three columns supporting the south facade (FLC 29128; the second column may be the one behind, though no other details behind the facade plane are shown in this drawing). Despite the numerous circumstantial adjustments, the result has the quality of a symbolic diagram.

of architecture as establishing the conditions for praxis – action and reflection.

Aujame and Meissonier, among others, describe Le Corbusier passing from drawing-board to drawing-board in the atelier: upon being unable to resolve a problem, he would turn away and remark, "L'architecture c'est difficile." Having worked the following morning on the problem in his studio at rue Nungesser et Coli, he would return to the atelier with what was called a 'hieroglyph'. This often changed the direction of the project radically; but the change was rarely for the sake of efficiency or ease of construction, but rather for the sake of the meaning of the edifice. The 'hieroglyph' was neither a theory nor a building, but rather a quasi-architectural diagram of intentions executed in coloured crayons, for the purposes of collaboration with a fellow-designer.

Architecture is indeed 'difficult'. Its most important aspects inherently resist theoretical determination. Once inhabited, it is always already-before, or 'older' than, whatever one is doing or thinking. Design requires not only an architectural imagination, but also cultural judgement – one's wit or tact, the sense of what is true, or of what matters in concrete circumstances. Le Corbusier referred to his highest intentions as 'poésie', probably with Mallarmé in mind, which indicates the communicative order to which he aspired. However, his poetics also account for his vacuous cities. This is a serious problem, for what is true is so for everyone; it has a collective or universal dimension that is the basis of any plausible communication. For most of Europe's history, the working horizon of universality has been one's city. Moreover, these universals are only secondarily expressed as concepts – they are rather the conditions that are always there for everyone. Unless one is God, these can only be taken up in particular circumstances in history.

Well before Le Corbusier, the city – more than architecture – had been the subject of an effort to mobilize urban culture for the sake of planning. That Le Corbusier's architecture more readily accepts the dialogical involvement with the given conditions is, therefore, typical of the period. However, he also believed that his architecture could be the vehicle of a species of transcendent understanding that no longer required the city (or enabled him to regard the city as a large building for the purposes of design).

In these terms, the Tower of Shadows at Chandigarh exists in a half-way world: it is an architectural element set within urban conditions – a park – largely established by Le Corbusier and his collaborators. Constructed more than a decade after his death from drawings (by Talati) that had reached an advanced stage, it is marvellously crude in both execution and conception. The board formwork of the rest of the capitol was used here, and we can only speculate on the possible inclusion of the reliefs or colour that customarily found their way into the late works during construction, and which tentatively populate the sketches for this area. Similarly, it has the quality of a symbolic diagram, not yet architecture, in part because the intended context is still incomplete.

It seems to have been conceived as the principal pedestrian portal to the Capitol Park, although this is not said in Last Works, where it was first published. However, its ramp leads up from an area ("The Pit of Consideration") opened to the main path from the city of Chandigarh (figs. 2, 3). The central esplanade of the Capitol Park can be attained only by passing up through the buildings, and the Tower of Shadows replicates this ascent (fig. 8). Moreover, whilst Talati's notes (FLC 5818/19) are entirely concerned with the capacities for the brise-soleil to produce shadow during the year, the absence of any brise-soleil in the north facade make the edifice a monumental gate framing views to the Himalayas, between Parliament and the Governor's Palace. The three benches placed in the southeast corner (fig. 10) make a vestibule at the arrival from the bridge and ramp, and re-enact the persistent theme at the Capitol Park of mountain and plain, of which the Tower itself is an example.

The tower-gate which opens into town or citadel is an archaic setting for important rituals and ceremonies, long recognized to stand for the town as a whole. Were it certain that Le Corbusier had in mind civic-gate themes, possibly on the inspiration of Indian examples – Muslim, Hindu or colonial – one might pursue a traditional analysis of such gates. For example, the square-rotated-within-a-square configuration of the plan (fig. 1) has been associated, since Plato's Meno, with anamnesis and metympsychosis, and therefore with the mediation between eternal and historical, divine and human. Similarly, the cardinal orientation of the Tower of Shadows suggests such prototypes as the Athenian Tower of the Winds, re-enacted in Vitruvius's wind-rose city. On this basis, one might offer that the Tower of Shadows strove to reconcile the transient and the particular (as a place of ascending or descending passage) with the more primordial or universal conditions of orientation. This material appears only in fragments, if at all, in Le Corbusier's writing and drawings; but it is, nonetheless, a fair summary of his intentions. Indeed, the edifice embodies the nucleus of architectural ordering for Le Corbusier.

Like the esplanade as a whole, the Tower of Shadows is part of the family of foyer-settings in his work. The most exquisite example of these, that of the Pavillon Suisse, displays the main characteristics: an ambiguous spatiality set in shadow from which one ascends to light. Elaborate foyers appear in the Baroque, but they acquire their modern character under the École des Beaux-Arts principle of *la marche*, whereby circulation both structures buildings and is the vehicle of perspectival effects. Corbusian foyers mark a transition between those of the École and the contemporary interest in concourses and flowspaces, which are seen to embody a species of freedom for bourgeois mass-culture. Enacted as a drama of wandering versus directed movement, 'circulation' is made to bear connotations of history, whose supposed purposeful advance might arise from the lost, or potential, times of the foyer. Such themes are prominent in Le Corbusier's *Le Poème de l'Angle Droit*, of 1953.

In his account of the foyer of the Pavillon Suisse in the *Œuvre Complète*, 1929–34, Le Corbusier speaks of the success at being able to compose with fragments. This in turn became a key aspect of the most important settings of his late architecture – such as the chapels at Ronchamp and La Tourette, the parliament chamber (fig. 4) and courtrooms at Chandigarh, the Philips Pavilion. Like the Tower of Shadows, these have a shadowy, cave-like aspect, are oriented about agonic situations (situations of conflict and decision) and display a precisely mediated ecstatic spatiality. This last phenomenon, in which violent forms are equilibrated by geometry and light, corresponds to "l'espace indicible", which *Le Poème de l'Angle Droit* (C.3) renders as:

> the harmony/ of times the penetration of/ forms proportion....
> preclud[ing]/ the control/ of/ reason/ carried beyond/ all/

2. Chandigarh, site plan (*Œuvre Complète*, 1957–61, p. 72). Tower of Shadows at centre. The solstice sculpture is shown here in an early version – open arcs and positioned at the edge of the pool.

3. Tower of Shadows, axonometric reconstruction rotated 90° clockwise from the plan above, looking northwest across the entry road into the Pit of Consideration towards the Tower of Shadows, with the solstice sculpture behind, Ramp of Martyrs to right.

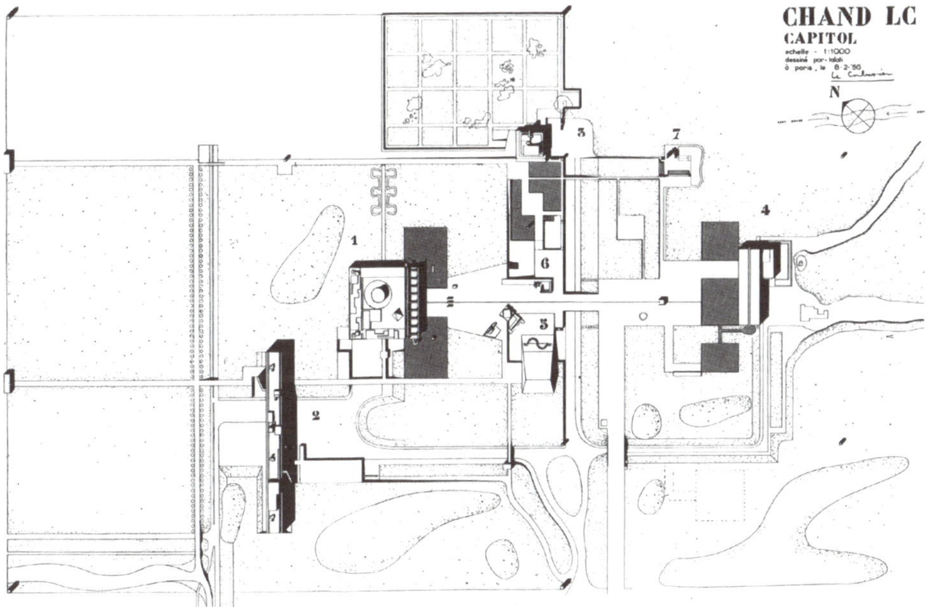
CHAND LC
CAPITOL
echelle - 1:1000
dessiné par - talati
à paris , le 8-2-56
N
1
2
3
4
5
6
7

> diurnal/ reality/ admitted/ to the heart/ of an/ illumination/
> God/ incarnate/ in/ the illusion/ the perception/ of truth/
> perhaps....

L'espace indicible, in turn, is the culmination of his conception of a *synthèse des arts*, a relic of the *Gesamtkunstwerk* which strives to synthesize the arts because they are deemed the receptacle of culture, or at least cultural values. In terms of what is true or what matters, therefore, it is for Le Corbusier an issue of synthesis ("harmony/penetration of times and forms...beyond reason") which obtains in a quasi-ecstatic experience ("an illumination... illusion... perception") of transcendence ("God incarnate..truth perhaps"). He renders this experience in terms of the extremes of representational possibilities: in terms of setting and of language (*l'espace indicible* roughly translates 'space beyond words').

The Romantic conception of the secular–sacred allows Le Corbusier to advance such a proposition. In the presentation of the project for a cavern-shrine of Mary Magdalene at Saint-Beaume in *Œuvre Complète, 1952–57*, he reproduces a segment of section C.2 of *Le Poème de l'Angle Droit*:

> ...the deep shelter is/ in the great cavern of/ sleep that other
> side of/ life in the night. How/ night is alive rich in the/
> warehouses collections/ libraries museums of/ sleep!

The cave is made the basis of commonality between secular repositories of 'culture' and the sacred shrine (in his work, Le Corbusier often presents the cave together with the tent, as he does in the lithographs for G.2 and G.4 of *Le Poème de l'Angle Droit*). Indeed, one sees as early as the Ozenfant House the motif of the dark cave-museum; and, from the Spiral Museum through the Pavillon des Temps Nouveaux to the Phillips Pavilion, its characteristic embodiment is the three-dimensional collage.

The most ambitious example is probably the ziggurat-mound of the Mundaneum, whose spiral descent through European culture would have admitted one to an eight-storey-high cavern with, at its centre, a 'shrine' to such fonts of creativity as Leonardo da Vinci. Even if one believes that this edifice is intended to be a Tower of Babel, a testament to the 'nightmare of history' which would be redeemed in the luminous shell of the League of Nations hall at the shore of the lake, the comprehensive programmatic disposition of cultural material is more than planning can legitimately encompass. The consequent didactic anxiety of this

4. Hall of Assembly, Chandigarh. An example of Le Corbusier's 'agonic' settings. Placed at the base of the hyperbolic shell and acoustic 'clouds', it is also a receptacle of cast and reflected sunlight from above.

enterprise, the grand theme of cultural renewal and rebirth, the fear of death and history and the ecstatic spatiality removed from the flux of everyday affairs, inspire Le Corbusier to indulge thoughts of 'synthesis' along with intimations of transcendence. In order that the agonic settings might achieve this, Le Corbusier combined the attributes of his museums with those of his foyers.

Like the Mundaneum and League of Nations project, the Capitol Park is set in nature. The idea that political debate would be secured in its authenticity through 'recovering' its roots in primordial nature is a familiar Enlightenment concept. This concept, however, subverts the original relation of *nomos* (law or custom) and *physis* (nature as ground of reality). Once the gods harboured by *physis* are abandoned, 'nature' becomes an aggregate of concepts depending upon the purposes or project, in this case to find what are imagined to be originary conditions, the orientation otherwise lacking in fractious post-eighteenth-century democracy. The Capitol Park's emancipation of political debate from its customary home in an urban setting (polis/politics) is therefore less inspired by Versailles or Lutyens's New Delhi than by Le Corbusier's concept of nature. This topic is more vast than can properly be treated here – it includes the 'laws of nature' supposedly the province of the engineer, 'natural' geometries, the cycles of tides and sun, the 'law of the meander', the 'axis of the cosmos', etc. The aspect which concerns us is a particular configuration of landscape.

Apparently influenced by the work of Appia, the central region of Chandigarh comprises recesses in the earth and an archipelago of architectural fragments and iconic signs, of which the Tower of Shadows is one. This plateau seems to be given over to contemplation in the presence of the horizon, and it is prefigured by the roof-gardens of, for example, the Villa Stein-et-Monzie at Garches or the Villa Savoye at Poissy. The variant developed for the Spiral Museum (supposedly to be set amongst 'beets and potatoes', presumably acknowledging the etymological relation between cult, cultivation and culture) orchestrates the ground in a complex play of buildings, trees, sculpture, planes and a rhythm of paths alternately straight and winding – all as preparation for ascent into the cave of the museum. A landscape both coming into being and passing away (reminiscent of a field of ruins), it is also the basis of his recurring play with interior and exterior horizons involving shelves, tables, beds, parapets, etc. Briefly, there seem to be two different purposes combined in the one motif. As it has its origins in the sets of Appia, it would seem to comprise a direct appeal to the earth, literally to 'ground' the otherwise conceptual operation of space as receptacle of references. Secondly, the proposition incorporates the horizontal conditions within the composition, and renders the intermediary domain as earth and geometry. The result provides something of a 'theatre of the world' for praxis: "...since you are upright [*droit* – the word carries both the moral and physical senses]/ you are fit for action. Upright on the terrestrial plateau of knowable things you/ sign a pact of solidarity/ with nature: this is l'angle droit" (A.3). The interaction of *l'angle droit* with nature is the nucleus of *l'espace indicible* and, with that, the experience of cultural synthesis.

Le Corbusier means to have it both ways – he wishes to make praxis accountable to transcendent conditions but he also wishes the outcome to be known in advance, through orchestration of 'grounded' meanings all the way to the horizon. The bourgeois remorse over the loss of meaning solves the problem by transferring everything to "the terrestrial plateau of knowable things". This requires a plateau as such – a *res extensa* – to be manifest literally within given nature; and this is not available in a city (although it is the constitutive feature of Le Corbusier's 'Radiant City', at the cost of any recognizable urbanity).

Only architecture can tangibly do this; and the laconic space of modernism has replayed the theme with endless variations, although only De Chirico and a Surrealist such as Ernst caught the tragedy of the proposition. Nor is it simply visual, incorporating the given horizon with several others in the three-dimensional collage. Rather the already-before of architecture becomes subsumed with that of nature to create a setting which speaks of primordial origins – so long as one assumes these origins to be a condition of emptiness awaiting civilization. Here the earth/ground is subject to a confusion of understanding, attempting to be both a diagrammatic space governed by formal rules and a setting for dramatic action, both a gameboard (or designer's blank sheet, with its protocols of planning and production) and a stage. The first is atemporal, sustaining 'moves' which are reversible and endlessly re-playable, whilst the second requires the particularities of character, choice and history (Le Corbusier presents *Le Poème de l'Angle Droit* in precisely these terms – as both the *iconostase*, a 'Tarot-deck' of icons, and as a narrative poem). To this extent, these topographies are like the post-Enlightenment monument, which strives through design to find a setting outside the claim of history. The structure of *Le Poème de l'Angle Droit* shows how Le Corbusier imagined this to be achieved – architecture (B.2-4) is positioned between natural cycles (A.1-5) and a human dialectic of aimless wandering and sexual intimacy (C.1-5), the latter providing the analogies for the rupture out of everyday existence into *l'espace indicible* through contemplation of the icons and signs which comprise the rest of the poem.

The temporal modalities of architecture are important to Le Corbusier. The zeitgeist or avant-garde or revolutionary aspects of this have attracted undue attention, since they are manifestations of the conventional and somewhat pathetic Enlightenment anxiety regarding history, consequent to presuming that we could take responsibility for everything. However, on pages 14-15 (A.1) of *Le Poème de l'Angle Droit*, Le Corbusier attempts to reinterpret traditional temporal and light symbolism (much as he transposed Pythagorean aural metaphors to optics for the sake of the Modulor). Traditionally, light has two opposites – darkness (which concerns moral or intellectual orientation) and matter (which concerns the structure of reality, from invisible to visible, typically represented through geometric metaphors). The first is psychological, the second ontological. Whereas traditional religion and philosophy see it a desideratum of great difficulty to reconcile the psychological and the ontological, the particular and the universal, Le Corbusier bypasses the difficulties by arguing through visual analogies. The four diagrams (fig. 5) make a series which progresses from the black-and-white striated stone in which Le Corbusier saw a self-portrait (a psychological metaphor) through a black stone inscribed with the geometry of the golden section (matter the receptacle of form, a metaphor for the order of reality) to the orbital dance of the planetary 'stones', each given a geometric designation, to the division of the solar year manifest as phases of day and night. This demonstration is called, "the furnishing of a measure... which regulates our destiny". "Measure" here carries three senses: the presence of difference as opposites (dark/light, matter/form, etc.), the structuring of difference harmonically, and its disclosure as temporal cycles "which regulate our destiny". History for Le Corbusier is a dialectic between confusion and truth (between deviation and assertion of straightness – *droiture* – according to A.4, the 'law of the meander'), which

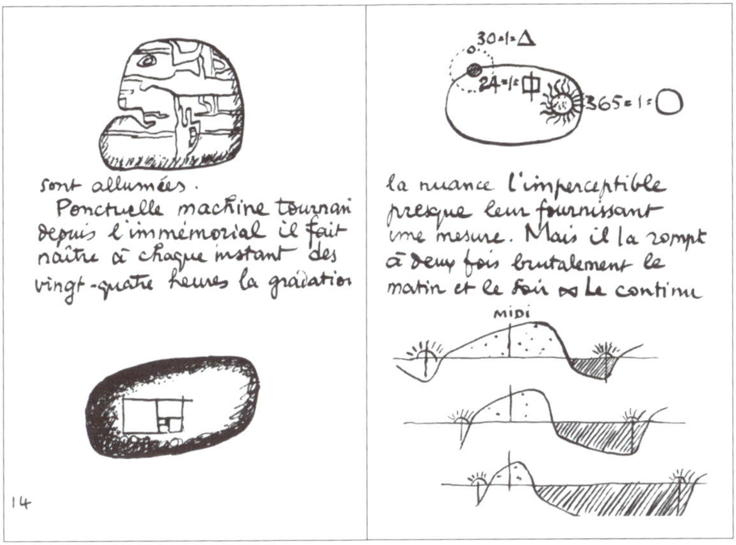

5. Pages 14–15 of *Le Poème de l'Angle Droit.*

6. Tower of Shadows, site plan reconstructed from FLC 29131, 29132 (as published in *Last Works*, p. 74, except the original axonometric has the solstice sculpture drawn in pencil). Shadows as cast at noon on the winter solstice. A right angle is created at the north face of the Tower.

transpires within the more permanent conditions articulated as "measure". This relation between history and the permanent conditions of 'measure' is embodied in his solar diagram, which presents the movement of the sun with respect to the "plateau of knowable things"; but the diagram is also, as it was for Le Corbusier's contemporary, Fulcanelli, an apocalyptic icon, signifying "a new time" (D.3). The area around the Tower of Shadows is furnished with several large solar icons, as well as a "Ramp of Martyrs" (fig. 7), whose role as an icon for history is made clear in FLC drawings 5815, 5818, 29131, where the transition from straightness to deviance is marked by a sculptural group (Ubu?), the "obstacle " which provokes the drama of the meander (A.4).

We may summarize our findings. The Tower of Shadows re-enacts the material embodiment of proportion as well as light/shadow. As one object among several disposed about the "plateau of knowable things" that is the esplanade – both gameboard and stage – the Tower of Shadows serves to invoke the dialectics of history and measure. As entry into this situation, it is encountered in a skewed milieu of obliques and shadows, from which one ascends to light orthogonally oriented, as is often the case in Corbusian foyers (fig. 8). In this respect, the esplanade is a species of 'roof garden' to which all the buildings of the Capitol Park provide the entry. As an edifice in its own right, the ascent up the ramp to a cave-like space of contemplation recalls the similar motif detected by Tim Benton in his studies of the Ozenfant House and Villa La Roche. Finally, the transparency of the Tower of Shadows emphasizes the complementarity of the agonic chambers and the world-theatre of the esplanade. One can appreciate that Le Corbusier has found in the Tower of Shadows' rhythmic frame orbiting about the central, full-height column and set within the mobile horizons of the Capitol Park an austere, minimum configuration for the movement towards *l'espace indicible*.

However, it is difficult to believe that this conforms entirely to the victorious language of "God incarnate…truth perhaps" of *Le Poème de l'Angle Droit*. One is alerted to a possible counter-theme by placing the Ramp of Martyrs – in itself a conventional enough sentiment of post-Romantic politics, both democratic and fascist – together with the sublime aesthetic death that the experience of *l'espace indicible* entails (beyond "the control of reason…[and] all diurnal reality"). To be sure, the affiliation of the sun with agonic themes is as old as Aristotle's dictum in the *Poetics*

7. Tower of Shadows, reconstructed axonometric looking southwest, on a late spring morning, with the sun aligned with the east facade of the brise-soleil. The illustration shows the penetration of sunlight on that day and the archipelago of architectural fragments and icons. The Ramp of Martyrs is to the left.

8. Tower of Shadows site, reconstructed perspective taken from the position of a person entering the Capitol Park through the Pit of Consideration and Tower of Shadows, morning sun, spring. The view is taken at esplanade level to show how one is positioned below the horizon of the solar diagram to the left. This horizon both stabilizes and contains a milieu of obliques and shadows. The Tower presents itself as an illuminated frame of shadow, through whose transparency the sky is visible, making a large window or portal at the head of the ramp.

that "tragedy should take place in a single circuit of the sun, or perhaps a bit more". However, it seems that, to Le Corbusier, the sun – "master of our lives/ distant indifferent..a seigneur" (A.1) – destroys the more benign condition of shadow.

In one important respect the Tower of Shadows is the intentional inverse of the agonic settings. These are virtually windowless, sealed realms, whereas the Tower of Shadows is all windows. However, the reticulated frame of the Tower is also the latent presence in the agonic settings, which tend to manifest their orthogonal order implicitly. The reciprocity of the two orders is played out in more equal terms at the Millowners' Building, itself a reprise of the Villa at Garches. Accordingly, what is latent in the agonic settings is explicit in the Tower – for which the circumambulating horizon marks the walls of its 'room' – appropriate to its preparatory role as a gate.

Because one first encounters the Tower from the south, it presents itself as a luminous frame containing a box of shadow, mysteriously carved out of the sky in broad daylight (fig. 8). Talati devoted much effort to securing not only shadow but also the penetration of sunlight during certain periods, particularly from the east and south, where the vertical members are oriented to admit light. A virtual, or shadow-architecture is a recurrent theme of the photographs Le Corbusier publishes of his buildings, the most monumental early example being that created in the great void of the Villa at Garches (complete with shadow-inhabitant). However, with the late works, a new variant appears, where the photographs create abstract patterns, often a play of pure rhythm (fig. 9). The reader of the *Carnet de la recherche* devoted to the chapel at Ronchamp is invited to rotate the photographs, thereby creating havoc with the traditional mediating interpretation of light. The proposition involves a *coincidentia oppositorum*, whereby that which establishes the firm frame of structure and proportionality is also responsible for its dissolution in an umbrous milieu of ambiguous spatiality. There are two themes operating at once. Firstly, the rhythmic patterning of darkness and light transfers the architecture to the realm of *l'espace indicible*, declaring what might be termed a potential architectural order, neither fully present nor utterly lost. Secondly, the element of explicit contradiction prevents reading the works in the purely Vitruvian terms of firmness, utility and beauty or, more generally, in terms of making culture a project of this

9. Secretariat, Chandigarh, under construction – an example of Le Corbusier's interest in 'shadow architecture' (*Œuvre Complète*, 1952–57, p. 84).

kind. Here the remorse at loss of meaning confronts the tragedy of attempting to recover it through the making of history or culture (through making *phronesis* – moral behaviour for its own sake – subject to *techne*, in the formulation of Gadamer). This either conforms to a supposed 'turn' in Le Corbusier's late work, or confirms the Tower of Babel in the Geneva project, depending upon the interpreter, or upon Le Corbusier's own uncertainty in the matter.

The use of architecture to create abstract patterns is not restricted to Le Corbusier, being, for example, a regular preoccupation of Bauhaus photography. The axonometric colour-patterns of Van Doesberg or Constructivism also indicate that it was part of the promise of 'space' to be weightless, a realm of emancipation. However, none of Le Corbusier's photographs or images are as abstract as those of De Stijl or Constructivism. This, coupled to the consistency with which Le Corbusier deploys shadow, and its inevitable connection to his solar themes, solicits the interpretation offered here. For Le Corbusier, the sun was not only a friendly Mediterranean play of light but also the principal adversary in a battle. This 'rage against the light' is, as he says, carried in the term 'brise-soleil', sun-breaker. He speaks of the 'brutal' division into day and night in *Le Poème de l'Angle Droit* (A.1). In general, the 'pitiless' clarity with which human affairs are exposed in sunlight – marked by the scepticism of one's colleagues: "everywhere we hear 'No!'" (D.3) – is contrasted with the shadowy potential for them to be otherwise. Positively, the symbol of the right angle is confected in darkness (G.3), as against the broken four-quartered circle associated with the upright man in sunlight at the beginning of the poem (A.3 – where also the earth contour mimics the curves of the solar diagram). The 'brutal division' into day and night is associated with the battle-imagery which characterizes the daylit struggle in *Le Poème de l'Angle Droit*. Whilst the two possibilities are always presented dialectically, their equality itself overturns traditional understanding. The most famous shadow-cave, in Book VII of the *Republic* of Plato, presents human affairs as the projections of puppet-shadows cast by fire, a weak surrogate for the blinding light of truth outside the cave. Following this analogy, we may ask whether Le Corbusier read this fire as the quest to mobilize culture through our representations, as the fatal attraction of 'synthesis', which can always only be provisional, confected on "the plateau of knowable things".

10. Tower of Shadows, reconstructed perspective from north, with no cast shadows – an otherwise impossible view because of the efficiency with which the edifice is filled with shadow. Two conflicts in the drawings have been resolved as follows: the minor horizontal members have been stopped at the southeast vertical member of the south facade (*contra* FLC 29128 and 29130, but *con* 29127 and as built); and a portion of the lowest minor horizontal has been removed to the southeast corner (neither in the drawings or as built), on the thesis that one was in fact supposed to enter the Tower of Shadows from the ramp without having to crawl or to pass through the corner, such a corner entry not being found in any other Corbusian building. According to FLC 29128 and 29130, neither is possible, raising the possibility that one was in fact supposed to walk around the building. However, such an ornamental ramp is not found elsewhere in Le Corbusier's work. Ramps are generally significant structuring elements of Corbusian buildings; and, in early versions of the Tower of Shadows (seen in the wooden model of the Capitol Park), the ramp went to the roof – a common starting-point for his buildings.

Given the importation into *Le Poème de l'Angle Droit* from Plato's *Symposium* the image of men and women created by splitting a sphere, and from the Philebus the Promethean gift of fire/geometry (although he cites Aeschylus in *Le Modulor*), my invocation of the Platonic cave may not be speculative. That, furthermore, we are in the presence of some sort of inversion of Plato's affiliation of (sun)light with truth might be read from the descent south to the noon sun from the Tower of Shadows (during which one passes through all points of the compass), as against the ascent to light from Plato's cave. Moreover, the loss of diurnal reason in *l'espace indicible*, embodied in the secular-sacred cave settings of the agonic chambers, seems an adequate rendering of the milieu of the shadowy dwellers of Plato's cave.

A preference for Dionysos over Apollo is older than Nietzsche; and one wonders if the issue here is not simply Corbusian frustration – that, a bit like the sexual intimacy which inspires the experience of *l'espace indicible*, the mystical synthesis of the right angle must generally be confined to darkness and personal sensation, somewhat embarrassing to the scrutiny of daylight. If so, is it the fault of the synthesis – too many private metaphors, perhaps, necessitating a sustained exercise of decoding or translation to understand, and manifesting a personal rather than a collective culture? What Le Corbusier regards a 'gift' is deemed arrogance by the rest of the world. Or does the problem lie less with the 'what' of Corbusian mythology than with the 'how' – that he expects the metaphors to have an effect on our lives? The tyranny of *poésie* is not to be distinguished from that of technology or any other representational reduction of life to a programme for accomplishment; and to be the object of one person's salvational utopia is always more evil than the evil that exists. However, it is worth recognizing that the remorse over the loss of meaning has inevitably been accompanied by the confidence to do something about it, and that this is generally undertaken through the very procedures which created the remorse – the mobilization of culture through concepts supported by statistical demographics or the equivalent in order to 'improve' health, leisure, education, even politics. In these terms, *poésie* is pathetic not because it frustrates the project of mobilization, as Adorno argued, but because it is part of this project, it is untrue. How not to be part of this project has itself become a project (the avant-garde) with its own protocols and objectives.

If the consummate synthesis of the Tower of Shadows also appears to be as hollow metaphorically as it is physically, this is not only because Le Corbusier sought to deploy avant-garde means to achieve monumental ends, as Teige said of the Mundaneum project. It is because 'art', avant-garde or otherwise, seems to be caught in a strange choice between the monumental (for the museum) or the disposable (for commerce), both of which exhibit a species of death-wish. Le Corbusier's exemplars are those of the schools – medieval towns, Greece, Rome and so forth, later supplemented by India; and all the ingredients were boiled in cubism. He rereads these exemplars, but he expects his readings to have the exalted status of received aesthetic concepts, himself to be a cultural institution and the Tower of Shadows to stand alongside the 'monuments' of ancient cultures. However, the latter were not monuments, and were made less by individual genius than by the cultures. It is too early to say whether globalization will wipe out culture in this sense or precipitate many new, more local concretizations of human possibilities (or, less promisingly, both together, after the fashion of the nineteenth-century revivals). Le Corbusier's effort to translate the particularities of existence into a manageable aesthetic programme of salvation is not so very unlike that of Herder, with, however, one significant difference. Le Corbusier spoke most eloquently and credibly through his architecture, not as a philosopher, theologian, or poet. If the Tower of Shadows remains something of a symbolic diagram – an 'icon' or 'sign' in Le Corbusier's accurate terminology – it alerts one to what is at stake in a setting so apparently minor as the kitchen of the Millowner's building. The issue here is less a preference for cooking, a down-to-earth activity soliciting pious thoughts of humility, than it is of human possibilities manifest through concrete involvement. The illuminated cave and horizon themes here qualify the background to a particular aspect of praxis, whereas, in the Tower of Shadows, all reality is brought to 'circulation' and contemplation. Perhaps this is appropriate for so important a gate; as with most contemporary architecture, the result is ambiguous. Most importantly, however, the insights embodied in the architecture command a respect that also radically challenges our confidence in the conceptual determination of reality.

Tim Benton

The 'petite maison de week-end' and the Parisian Suburbs

This essay concerns a project that, although little known in the context of Le Corbusier's œuvre, is particularly illuminating about his attitudes towards the suburbs and suburban living. Designs for the Villa Félix or 'petite maison de week-end' (fig. 1), situated in the Parisian suburb of La-Celle-St-Cloud, were first drawn up in late 1934 and the house was built between April and June 1935. The authorship was divided between Le Corbusier and Pierre Jeanneret, his cousin and partner. By this time the two men, who had practised together for twelve years, were approaching domestic architecture in quite different ways. The designs for this house provide a privileged insight into these differences.

Like many architects in the 1920s and 1930s, Le Corbusier was drawn to the challenges – both in terms of architecture and planning – posed by Paris's growing outer suburbs or *banlieue*. It was only in the early twentieth century that this area became subject to widespread development following a housing crisis in the city centre. While many people had owned a small plot of suburban land (*lotissement*) in the suburbs, the codification in 1922 of a string of housing laws – collectively known as the Loi Ribot – aimed at persuading these people to become permanent residents by building their own homes. This had little effect and in 1928 another law was passed, the Loi Loucheur, which released substantial sums of money in the form of loans to potential suburbanites. Around 60,000 people in the Parisian suburbs made use of these new loans, which made a small contribution to the end-stage in the life of a suburban plot.[1] Typically a *lotissement* would have been purchased as an allotment, probably with a garden shed and a shelter for weekends, later developing into a hut or wooden shack where the family could stay for much of the summer. Later the shack could be converted into a permanent home for the family, made of brick or stone. This is where the Loi Loucheur came in.

The subsequent growth of the *banlieue* was tremendous. By 1931 there were 571,000 commuters – five times as many as in 1900.[2] However, the Loi Loucheur was far from universally popular and was seen by many to be politically motivated – a way of buying off would-be communists by turning them into working-class freeholders.[3] Moderate socialists on the other hand, with their belief in the benefits of the garden city,

1. Le Corbusier and Pierre Jeanneret, Villa Félix ('petite maison de week-end'), La-Celle-St-Cloud, Paris, 1935. Living room, view towards garden and bedroom (*Œuvre Complète*, 1934–38, p. 124).

welcomed the law, seeing it as an opportunity for the workers to take control of their futures and enjoy a healthier lifestyle. The rapid growth also brought with it significant problems, including the plight of the small house-owners who were let down by speculators and were known as '*mal-lotis*'.[4] Indeed, of the 500,000 new residents in the *banlieue* between 1921 and 1946, half were deemed *mal-lotis*.

French architects in the 1920s and 1930s tended to divide into three groups on the issue of the *banlieue*: those who thought it was a catastrophe, beyond salvation and fit only for abolition; those who saw it as a political question (that with proper planning a better way of life might be provided through social housing); and those who thought of it as a desert, a non-place, a literal utopia, a paradise of individualism and eccentricity, where you could do what you wanted – including modern architecture.

For the more conservative supporters of the French *régionaliste* style, such as Léandre Vaillat, Camille Mauclair and Gustave Umbdenstock, the banlieue was proof that ordinary people wanted natural materials, craftsmanship and 'homely' qualities.[5] Furthermore, the *banlieue* offered employment for the masons and stone cutters, the so-called *hommes du tas*, who seemed to them to represent the last bastion against the encroachment of the machine, communism and worse.[6] Most modern architects, on the other hand, condemned the *banlieue*, root and branch, as a breach of rational planning, an anarchy of selfish individualism and reactionary bad taste. The debate about the social, psychological and political effects of the '*enfermement pavillonnaire*', the '*rêve pavillonnaire*' and conservative individualism has continued into contemporary French housing literature;[7] indeed, the entire history of French housing from the turn of the century to the Second World War can be seen as an oscillation between English garden city notions and German and Russian social housing.

A fascinating insight into the psychology of the *banlieue* can be found in Blaise Cendrars' 1949 book, *La Banlieue de Paris*.[8] Cendrars loved to trudge across the 'maquis' of the *banlieue*, botanizing the various tribes of the Parisian suburbs, just as he had explored the Brazilian jungle. The book begins with Cendrars' attempt to visit Erik Satie at his home at Arcueil-Cachan. Satie, the 'best of the French modernists' ... 'a communist already in 1917', 'with not an ounce of snobbism in him', 'fiercely protected his independence from his friends and visitors from the city'. He never answered the bell. And this, for Cendrars, was 'the typical frame of mind of the *banlieusard*'.[9] The author is also sensitive to the daily tragedy of suburban isolation: 'A crazy world, which has had it, all washed up, in a mess, betrayed, a world of materialism, unfair, hard, wicked, a world of dog eats dog, a disgusting world; I was going to say a world without humanity, but that would be wrong.'[10] He railed at the horror of the little houses, fuelled by the hysterical love of nature and the compulsion to own something, built on endless scrimping and saving and sordid economies just to reach the final goal: to have one's own villa! 'Absurd, bizarre, self-righteous, uncomfortable, hideous, ridiculous, nightmarish, pretentious, clichéd. Never mind, we made it!' And Cendrars exposes the smug and 'satisfied' nature of these little homeowners in their little 'nests' and 'dun-roamins'.[11] Le Corbusier – who had corresponded with Cendrars in the past – would probably have echoed these thoughts fairly precisely.

But the spirit of optimism often prevailed in the pioneers of the *lotissements*. Listen to 'Madame G.', from Coudreaux:

> My father bought this scrap of land to go fishing in the lake.... The first house was this little wooden hut made of planks...Dad did it all, he was a carpenter-cabinet maker.... There were no roads, no nothing, only the woods; those really were heroic times. The wooden hut was never destroyed, it's still there inside, walled in by Italian bricklayers, the Cavinis.[12]

Now that's a foundation myth to which Le Corbusier might have warmed. In his moving account in *Une Maison un Palais* of the fishermen's houses in the pine forests of the Bassin d'Arcachon, Le Corbusier noted 'the isolation, the separation from the rest of the world' of the tongue of sand dunes, between the lagoon of Arcachon and the Atlantic. The fishermen, who worked there in the summer, 'only came there with the idea of living 'from day to day'. This precariousness put them into the paradigmatic situation of the house builder: they are making a shelter for themselves, somewhere to live, no more, in all simplicity and honesty. They are carrying out a pure programme unencumbered with claims to history, to culture, to the taste of the day. They're building a shelter, somewhere to live, with the materials that come to hand.'[13] And suddenly, says Le Corbusier, he realized that these houses were Architecture (or as he puts it, they were 'palaces'). There are other signs of Le Corbusier's preference for the most simple and primitive conditions for relaxing and living in the summer. On 10 July 1932 he had sketched a wooden shack, raised on stilts, rented by friends of his for a vacation. He notes: 'life enfolds entirely under the pilotis...' and he clearly considered this unbuttoned existence idyllic.[14] The suburbs could have been like this for Le Corbusier – a place for seeking the simple life in the internal frontier of the urban hinterland. Instead, he saw his role as that of forcing his 'poor little rich clients' (to use the phrase of Adolf Loos) into the straight-jacket of his architectural vision. They were given works of architecture but not necessarily the homes that either they or even Le Corbusier himself would have chosen to live in. And his projects for working people were from the outset conceived of as 'cells'.

Le Corbusier's involvement with the *banlieue* began in the early 1920s with his design for the Citrohan houses (1920 and 1922) and the apartment units of the 'Immeuble Villa' blocks of flats. This cell-type construction retained all of the functions of bourgeois life, including the key psychological ingredient, a garden (fig. 2). It was constructed at the 1925 exhibition, as the Esprit Nouveau Pavilion, and was explicitly advertised for sale as a suburban house, a standard type that could be built almost like an automobile. It also formed the basis for other private villa commissions such as the Villa Stein de Monzie, or the Villa Meyer project.

Another 'product' house was drawn up in direct response to the Loi Loucheur. Le Corbusier was an acquaintance of Louis Loucheur, the instigator of the law, and was consulted by him in the autumn of 1928. Le Corbusier's response to the law was a house-type that could be built by local builders without any sort of planning control and which he called the Maison Loucheur. The project went through a number of transformations as if to prove the flexibility of its design – one version included a downstairs atelier for would-be craftsmen – and it was conceived so that it could adapt to the typical pattern of growth for a *lotissement* as described earlier on. It was based on a steel frame box clipped onto a thick stone wall, the latter detail an explicit concession to local building industries.

Le Corbusier clearly thought that his Maisons Loucheur might spring up all over the suburbs, in response to need and supported by the funds provided by the Loi Loucheur. In fact not one was built, but Le Corbusier

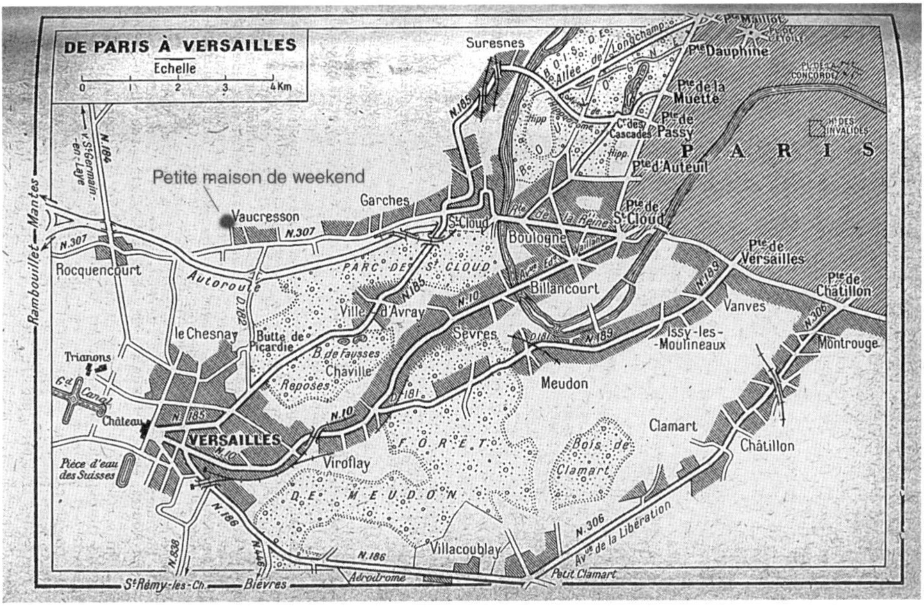

2. 'Springtime walk: if you're good ... we'll take a turn round the garden.' Cartoon published by Le Corbusier in *Une Maison un Palais*, p. 25.

3. Plan of western approach to Paris, from *Guide Bleu*, 1952.

did design three houses for named clients using the same basic principles. Of these, the Villa de Mandrot at Le Pradet, near Toulon was the only one to be constructed. Although the final form of the house was quite different to the first project (which was based on the Maison Loucheur), we can still see an echo of the underlying idea of the Maison Loucheur in the juxtaposition of rough stone walls and prefabricated, industrialized window fittings made by the Parisian firm Barriaux.[15]

In the 1920s and 1930s Le Corbusier was also involved in a number of other suburban villa projects, including Villa Meyer (designed 1925), Villa Stein de Monzie (commissioned 1925/completed 1928), Villa Cook (1926/1927) and Villa Savoye (1928/1931). Needless to say, Le Corbusier's Purist villas were not to be found in the Red Belt – made up of the communist-controlled arrondissements – around Paris, nor in the outlying settlements of pioneer houses, often called the 'Wild West' of the *lotissements de banlieue*. Instead they were situated along a royal/imperial axis which extends from the Louvre, along the Champs Elysées, Boulogne, Vaucresson, Garches, Ville d'Avray and La-Celle-St-Cloud to the park of Versailles (and beyond to Poissy and the forest of Rambouillet). In contrast to the eastern suburbs, this western approach is often referred to as the green, or more simply, rich, suburb (fig. 3).

These clients had cars, their sites were serviced with water and electricity and the roads had been metalled; they therefore shared nothing of the experience of typical suburbanites. The villas can be thought of as a series of bridgeheads in Le Corbusier's campaign to take over Paris; they took nothing from the suburb and gave nothing back. You could call it a 'bugger you' approach to the social and physical context. The Villa Stein de Monzie – set right back along its private road, protected by a gatehouse and a sliding metal gate, hidden behind abundant vegetation – is a good example. These are people who didn't care what the neighbours thought. And that's the point. You couldn't do this in Paris. The suburbs offered the conditions for individualistic self-expression.

So in the 1920s, Le Corbusier was operating in two quite different ways in the suburbs. On the one hand he was the champion of the 'product' house; on the other hand he was the architect of exclusive one-off villas. And his writings on the suburbs offer another angle again: 'Suburban life is a despicable delusion entertained by a society stricken with blindness!'[16] He records how his secretary explained her life to him:

spending hours on the train, living with her mother in the suburbs, bored out of her wits at the weekend, never meeting anyone. 'The martyrdom of suburbanites. And something else again: the terrible solitude in the crowd of that vast urban agglomeration. Oh, Liberty!'[17]

It is fair to say that, in spite of his awareness of the social problems that the development of the *banlieue* brought and his involvement with Loucheur, Le Corbusier's commitment was first and foremost to architectural rather than social solutions. In this he ran against the leaders of the Modern Movement; he was not a Lurçat, a Beaudouin nor a Lods, nor a Teige, a Van Eesteren or a Stam. At the 1929 CIAM meeting in Frankfurt, Le Corbusier was the only one to provide house designs, rather than flatted accommodation. The Maison Loucheur – while democratic in the sense that it was conceived as a product and mass produced like an automobile – was a far cry from communal living.

But Le Corbusier's flirtation with the individualistic product-solution was short-lived. By 1930, at the Brussels CIAM, he would have nothing more to do with garden cities (and hence the *banlieue*): 'The garden city leads to individualism. In reality to an enslaved individualism, a sterile isolation of the individual. It brings in its wake the destruction of social spirit, the downfall of collective forces'.[18] This was a standard line taken by housing reformers,[19] and in his book *La Ville Radieuse* (1933) Le Corbusier would simply have eliminated the garden city – 'a pre-machinist utopia' – and with it the suburbs.

While Le Corbusier may have turned his back on the garden city he did not lose his early fascination with vernacular and natural materials – stone, wood, brick, stucco – and the effects of texture and warmth that could be created with them.[20] *La Ville Radieuse* begins with the words: 'I am attracted to a natural order of things'. And Bruno Reichlin and others have written on Le Corbusier's 'discovery' of natural materials around the time of the Villa de Mandrot (1929–32) and possible links with the regionalist style.[21] One of his tropes of contentment (paradise on earth) was the medieval stone houses which his friend Badovici (and Eileen Gray) had opened up and refurbished in Vezelay. Pierre Jeanneret, Charlotte Perriand and Fernand Léger had also become very interested in the vernacular and the simple life which, together with left-wing politics, utopian primitivism and a touch of sexual spice between Pierre and Charlotte, provided a heady mixture.

But, how could Le Corbusier rescue natural materials from his sworn enemies in the *Style Régionaliste?* The answer lies in the notion of *objets trouvés or objets à réaction poétique*. The avant-garde could rehabilitate the vernacular only if it was stripped of its nationalist and traditionalist associations and rediscovered as a fragment of 'nature'. A modest building material which can be seen everywhere in Paris, and which was quarried in the suburbs, were moellons, mid-sized rubblestone blocks, of second quality, small enough to be carried up ladders. They can be found wherever they are meant to be invisible, in functional retaining walls, or when a party wall has, for some reason, been left exposed. These aren't the dressed ashlar stones of the Beaux-Arts architects, or the picturesque rusticated blocks of the *Style Régionaliste*. The moellon was a modest, simple, honest, local material. Le Corbusier liked to say that he had 'discovered' the beauty of the material in the party wall of his neighbour at rue Nungesser et Coli (actually a block of flats designed by Michel Roux-Spitz), with its characteristic red veins produced by the chimney flues, and had left it exposed, a pure and noble feature of his atelier.[22] This sign of 'the natural' also worked as an icon of the 'homely' and was built into the design of the house for Albin Peyron's son at Mathes and the 'petite maison de week-end', for Monsieur Félix at La-Celle-St-Cloud.

On the railway line from Saint-Cloud to Marly-le-Roi, passing Garches-Marnes-la-Coquette and Vaucresson you come to Bougival-La Celle-St-Cloud, 1.5km from La-Celle-St-Cloud (see fig. 3). The 1952 *Guide Bleu* describes it as a pretty village surrounded by chestnut forests on a hill. It was here that Félix bought his plot.

The project has the classic elements of a suburban home and the venture began according to type. An unidentified architect was asked to draw up what could only be called a regionalist dacha, in brick and fake half-timber (fig. 4), and this was granted building approval on 18 September 1934.[23] The original plan is of a minimal interior with living space, kitchen and bathroom downstairs and a mezzanine floor above for a bedroom. However, for whatever reason, this initial plan was discarded, and Le Corbusier and Pierre Jeanneret were given the commission.

The project was described as a caretaker's house and seems to have been built at the expense of Félix's company, La Société Henfel. Possibly this involved a tax dodge or cheating the shareholders; Félix later wrote to Le Corbusier: 'For special reasons, I must ask you not to discuss this

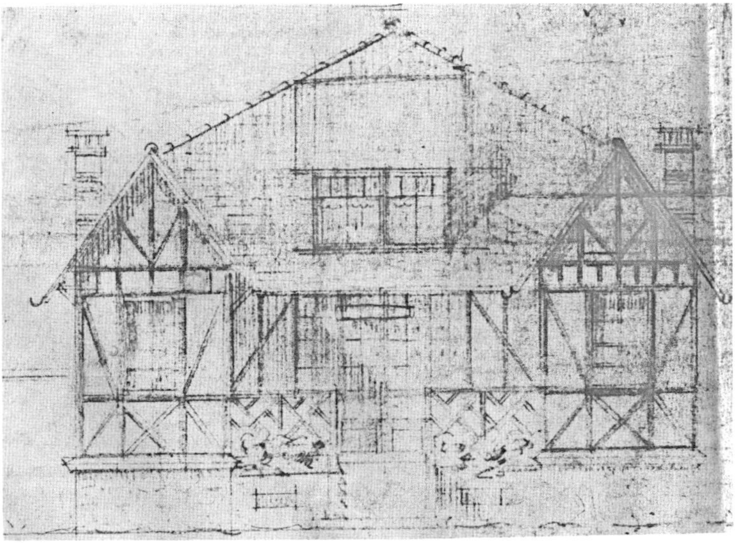

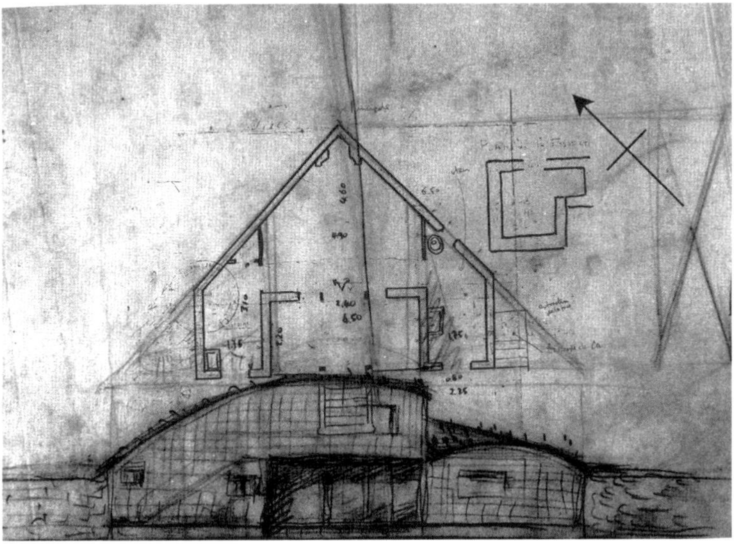

4. Southwest elevation by an unknown architect of cottage to be built on the plot of M. Félix, approved 18 September 1934 (FLC document H2-19 152).

5. In red, the plan by an unknown architect for a half-timbered cottage to be constructed in the northeast corner of M. Félix's property, 18 September 1934 (FLC document H2-19 152). In grey, Pierre Jeanneret's sketch plan and elevation (FLC 9265).

house, especially in the Gironde [where Le Corbusier was holidaying at the time], because I have business dealings down there'.[24] Who knows Félix's motives? The house was pinned back to the corner of the site, turning its back to the neighbours in approved suburban fashion and shrinking from the road. It is obvious that Félix, like Satie, defended his privacy tenaciously. It is important that the sacred secrecy of the suburb should not be disturbed. The key thing is that all the elements of suburban existence are brought together in this brief: the search for a simple life away from the hurly-burly of Paris – privacy and secrecy and a little house to match (informal, a bit quaint, unpretentious).

For the sake of simplicity, the projects are here divided into two main parts, with an intermediary phase. The first project, exclusively by the hand of Pierre Jeanneret, was drawn up before 13 December 1934 on a triangular *parti*. These plans and elevations could be characterized as a kind of modernist reflection on the suburb, in the context of the Front Populaire. On 13 December 1934 Le Corbusier had a meeting with Félix, after which he made a series of interventions which, via the intermediary phase, led to the final, and significantly more monumental, zigzag solution.[25] The finished building incorporates the new interest in natural materials, utilizing rubble stone walls with plywood lined interior surfaces, earth and grass on the roof and a landscaping which seeks to bed the house down into the soil. But this project also reveals Le Corbusier's characteristic disdain for the suburban context, with a bank of earth introduced to hide the house from the street.

Of the triangular plans initially drawn up by Pierre Jeanneret, only FLC 9265 follows the layout of the original plan (by the unidentified architect) exactly. It does this not only in the positioning on the page – with the bottom of the sheet oriented southwest – and the use of tripartite division, but also in the preservation of the symmetry around the angle of the corner. Superimposing the original scheme by the unknown architect in red on FLC 9265 shows the dependency of the latter – in plan but not in elevation – on the layout of the original simple suburban cottage (fig. 5).

This plan (FLC 9265) is schematic, divided into three, with a porch in the centre, like the original, but with the staircase on the left and the facade extended sideways to meet the garden walls. One vault covers the left and central bay (rising to cover the mezzanine bedroom), while the vault on the right is single storey. The parti can be seen quite clearly if the original plan is superimposed on Pierre's worked up version, FLC 9273 (fig. 6). In this, the facade has been tilted sideways towards the west, perhaps to accommodate a tree which was in the way on the west corner. A peculiar consequence of this displacement is that the cosy fireplace previously in the corner comes out on the elevation a third of the way along the facade and that the central axis of the facade comes out 2.50m along the right-hand wall. A little sketch on the same plan shows a rectilinear treatment of the roof. In FLC 9268 (not illustrated), this is worked up into a 'rationalized' version of the curvilinear facade, but then the idea is immediately dropped. Pierre seems to be determined to maintain a casual, organic form for the little house. The southwest facade as seen in FLC 9269 (not illustrated) shows traces of the erased rectilinear facade.

This asymmetrical, directional, curved facade offers a dynamic vision of modernity, with some of Pierre's dry humour in it. If, to Stanislaus von Moos, Citrohan I looked like a 10HP Citroën, this can be seen as a more streamlined updated version of the car. One of the clichés of life in the *lotissements* were the caravans and converted railway carriages – poignant symbols of transience and impermanence. In the plan FLC 9276 [not illustrated], Pierre transposes the chimney to the east wall, to bring it into the central axis of the facade.

Until now, all the plans have followed the original layout of the first project on the sheet. From FLC 9266 (fig. 7), the plan is turned round to align the facade with the bottom of the paper. The staircase is moved to the right and the porch consequently shifts to the left, towards a symmetrical alignment with the fireplace and its chimney (now again in the corner). This could be read as the first steps towards a more formal, hierarchic and symmetrical variant.

Round the edge of the drawing is an interesting study of intersecting vaults, which probably represents an intervention by Le Corbusier on the theme of how to light this awkward triangular space. His solution is similar to the sketch he made in 1928 labelled '*ma maison*', which differentiated a south-facing office from an accommodation block and studio space illuminated by north-facing windows contained in concrete vaults. A similar lighting solution would be found for his penthouse studio apartment in rue Nungesser et Coli. The pattern of alternating triangular

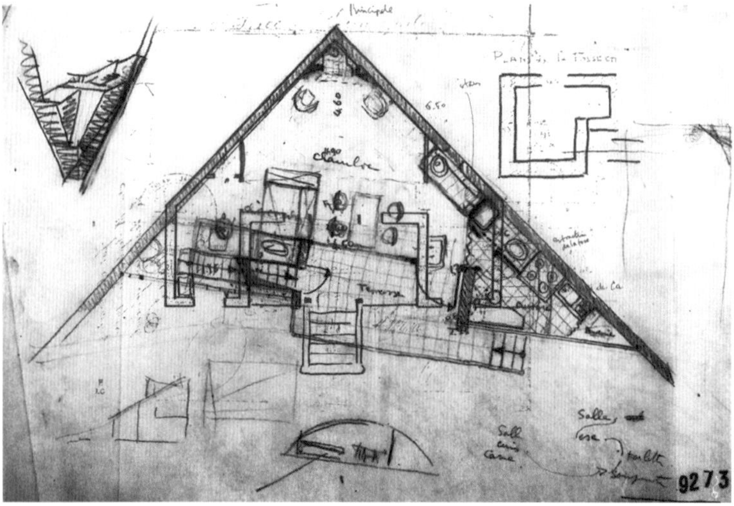

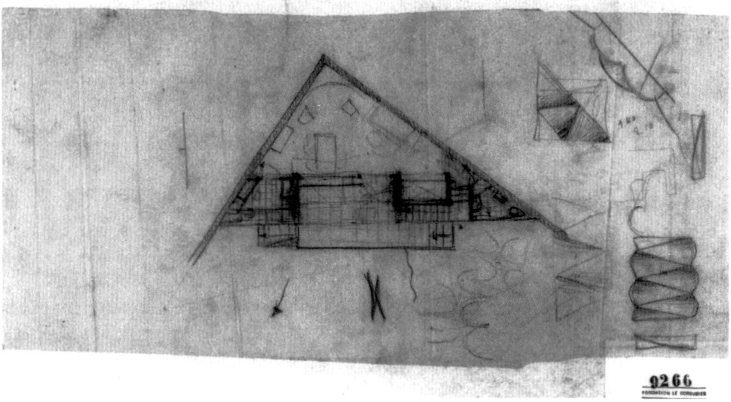

6. In grey, Pierre Jeanneret, development of the first project (FLC 9273); in red, the original plan by an unknown architect (FLC document H2-19 152).

7. Pierre Jeanneret, revision of the first project to align the facade with the paper and transpose the staircase (FLC 9266).

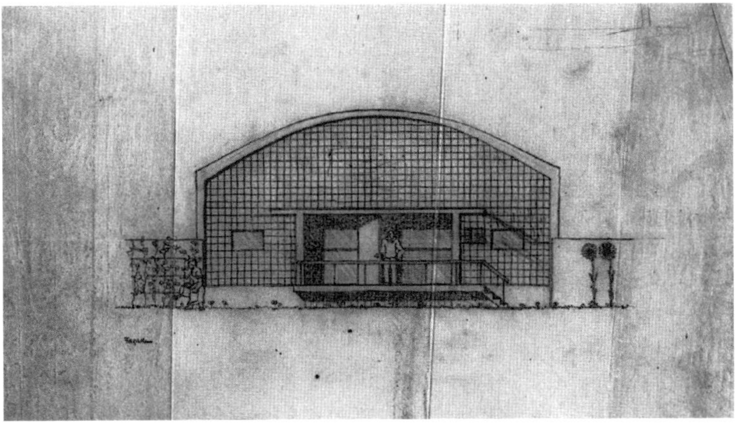

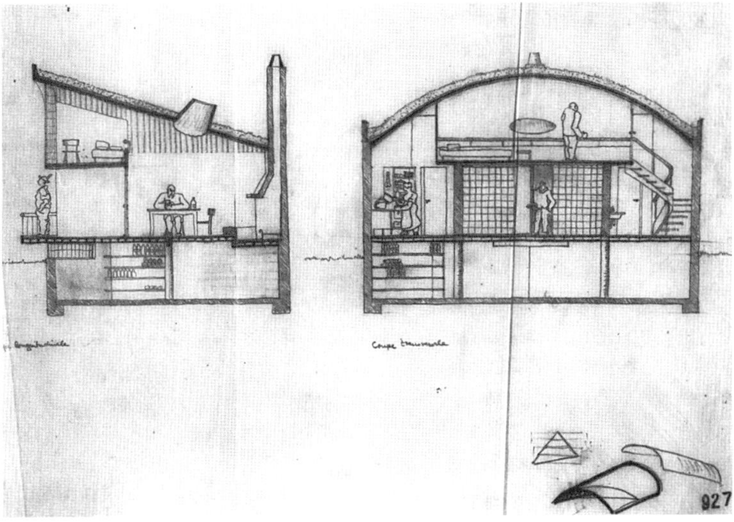

8. Pierre Jeanneret, southwest elevation, symmetrical variant of the first project, populated with avant-garde suburban pioneers (FLC 9278).

9. Pierre Jeanneret, long and short sections of symmetrical variant of the first project (FLC 9277).

vaults also leads towards a solution (sketched top right on FLC 9266) in which there is a single vault facing southwest, with a north-facing dormer. This in turn gets rid of Pierre's dynamic asymmetry of one large and one small vault to find a symmetrical facade. This symmetry is confirmed in the elevations and sections, FLC 9278 (fig. 8) and FLC 9277 (fig. 9), which mark the end of this series of drawings by Pierre Jeanneret.

So, the project returns to where it started – a symmetrical facade with a central *in antis* porch. Bye-bye to the suburbanite's car, hello to a kind of universal shed-hut. But who are the people Pierre has drawn in on his elevation and section: the bearded man in the worker's smock and his companion tending to her sweet peas? And look at those sunflowers, stereotype of the garden city ideal, signifying a life of natural growth under the sun's rays. Indeed, isn't the whole house a kind of sunflower, turning its face of Nevada glass tiles to the southwest? Is it Félix's dream of suburban life we see here, or Pierre's, peopled with Bakunian intellectuals, socialist ramblers, some chums who have bicycled over for the day and a young, pretty comrade cooking up the spaghetti? Above all, Pierre's project can be seen as an optimistic take on the *banlieue*. This is an image of a social avant-garde paradise, like that of Badovici's houses in Vezelay, or that of Norbert Bezard (the farmer from the Sarthe) debating the future of agriculture with Le Corbusier in the *Ferme Radieuse* (1934–5), while his vigorous, pretty and fertile young wife cooks dinner and the children play in the vegetable patch.[26]

An evocative but mysterious drawing, FLC 9270, forces an engagement with these speculations (fig. 10). This emblematic image might be called '*l'homme de pierre*' – the man of stone but also Pierre's man. This is the well-muscled and politically engaged man of the future, the man of the Front Populaire or '*l'homme réel*' (politically left or right). It belongs with the penultimate phase of the design, when the space heating was provided by a proletarian stove rather than a bourgeois fireplace.[27] He stands there, demonstrating the new order, a marriage of industry and craftsmanship, cast iron, brick and stone. The same yellow stone blocks and red bricks can also be found in the drawings for Mathes and, of course, in the studio penthouse at rue Nungesser et Coli.

As built (see fig. 1), the Villa Félix has a fireplace, with its associated primitivist art work in a niche: a cliché of bourgeois possession. It was Henri Frugès who had advised Le Corbusier in 1925 to put fireplaces into

10. Pierre Jeanneret, drawing of worker, wall of moellons, store and brick flue, associated with the intermediate project, January 1935 (FLC 9270).

the houses in Pessac, rather than the more efficient stoves, because he said that he couldn't feel 'at home' without the comfort of a real fire.[28]

After 13 December everything tightens up pretty quickly. FLC 9286 (fig. 11) acts as a dialogue between Pierre and Le Corbusier. Pierre appears to be explaining his project, with its elevation, while they explore the potential for different forms of vaulting (picking up the discussion from FLC 9266, see fig. 7). Le Corbusier seems to be referring to Gaudí and the Sagrada Familia school, which he had sketched, and also possibly to the Colonia Güell chapel. And, towards the top on the right-hand side, a version of the step-back solution is indicated. This is worked up into the bird's-eye view seen in FLC 9307 (fig. 12), which is labelled 'Casa Gaudí' and could be described as the 'intermediate' phase. Two other versions of this plan exist (FLC 9282, 9280), radically different to each other in appearance and culture. One of the versions, FLC 9282, has the appearance of a modest shack (and might be read as a return to the cottage origins of the project), while the other (FLC 9280) begins to develop a language of monumental vaulted spaces, illuminated with Nevada glass tiles.

The plan underlying each of these three very different external forms, FLC 9305 (fig. 13), is identical. Interestingly, the plan was probably traced over the lines of the original scheme, reverting to the alignment of the unknown architect's plan. The upper storey is now along the east wall, with access stairs on this wall, but the plan itself has become orthogonal, with an L-shape along the east and north garden walls of the property, framing a partially covered terrace towards the southwest. Comparing this with the earlier triangular plan is instructive. The new plan, FLC 9305, makes difficulties for itself with its large terrace which cramps the internal space. The next stage, FLC 9301 (fig. 14) is to turn the paper around again and align the east wall with the edge of the paper. In this plan, part of the terrace is occupied to make a large internal space of around 6m squared.

The next stage involves losing the upper storey, extending the east wing to the south to make a bedroom and squeezing everything else in. This is visible in FLC 9299, which was drawn before 4 January 1935 (fig. 15). On 4 January, Le Corbusier visited Félix again, and made a little sketch in his diary.[29] The emphasis was on building up barriers of earth to protect from the view from the street. A similar intervention can be seen on FLC 9299. At this point the vaults rested on steel or very thin concrete pilotis

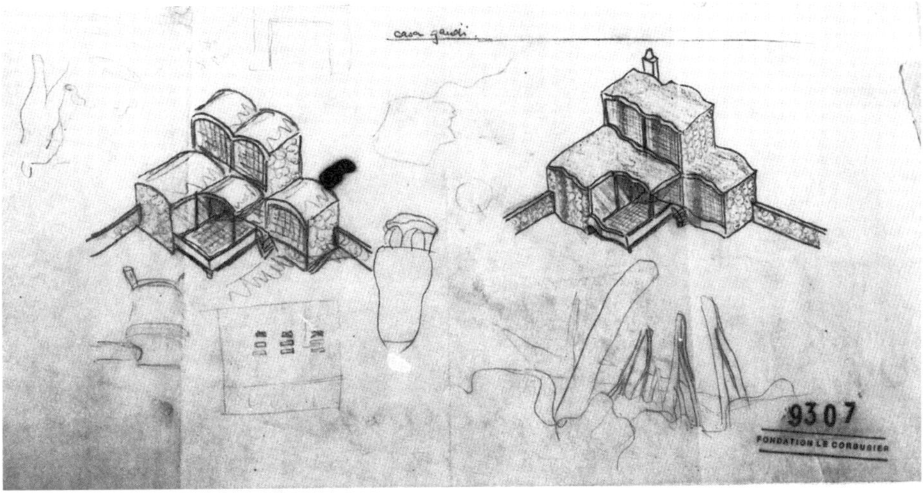

11. Le Corbusier and Pierre Jeanneret, sheet of sketches comparing the triangular first project with the step-back intermediate project, December 1934 (FLC 9286).

12. Pierre Jeanneret, two variants ('Casa Gaudí') of the intermediate project, December 1934 (FLC 9307).

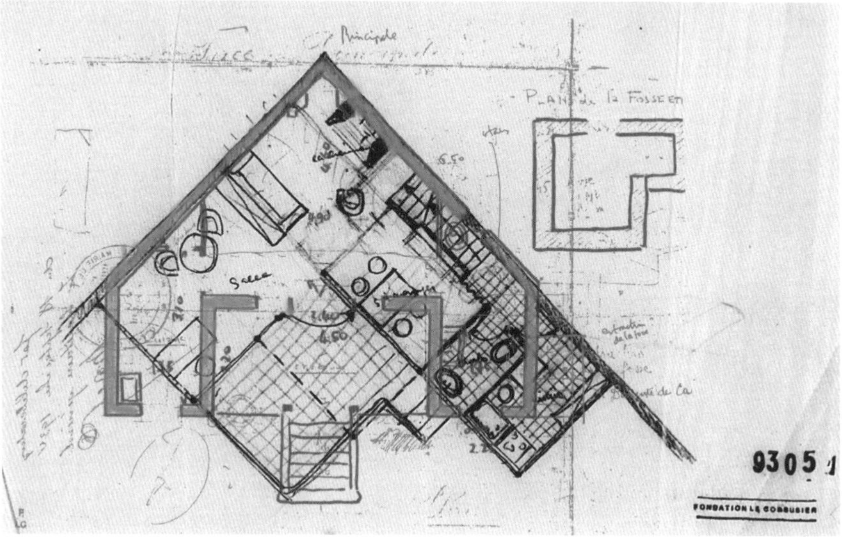

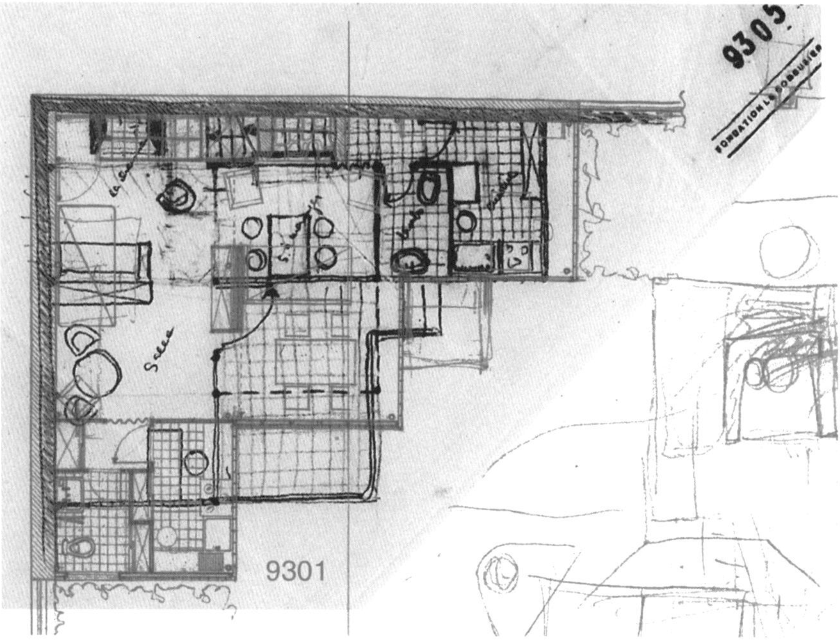

13. Comparison between the plan of the intermediate project (FLC 9035) and the original plan by the unknown architect (based on document H2-19 152).

14. Comparison between plan of the intermediate project (FLC 9305) and the first of the variants for the final scheme (FLC 9301).

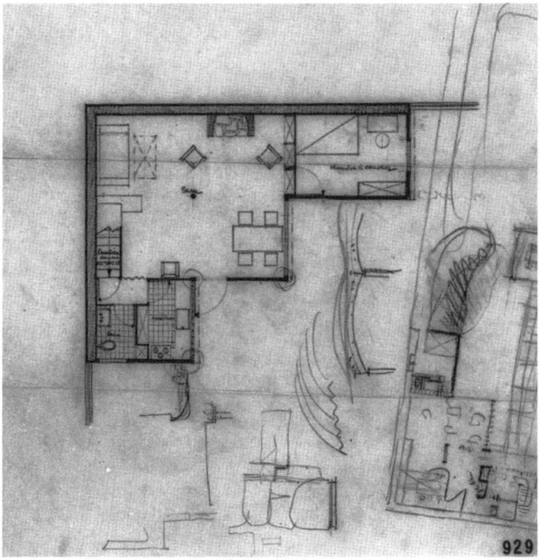

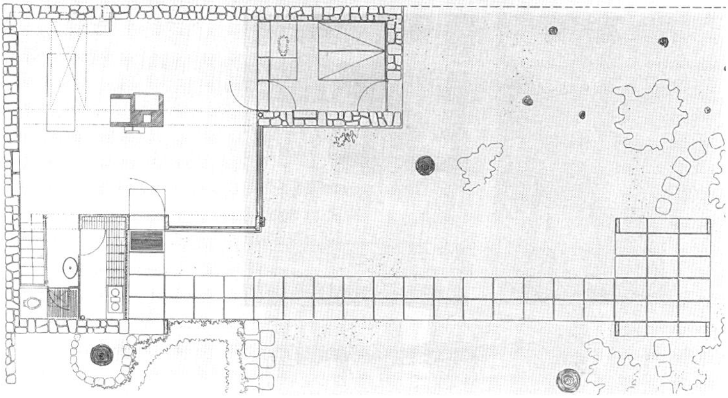

15. Pierre Jeanneret, pilotis variant of plan for the final project, with intervention by Le Corbusier indicating earthworks and garden layout, January 1935 (FLC 9299).

16. Le Corbusier and Pierre Jeanneret, plan of Villa Félix as built (*Œuvre Complète*, 1934–38, p. 125).

set inside the stone walls. These were shortly replaced by a system of stone walls (composed of moellons) and hidden steel supports framing Nevada glass tiles. What was left was a system of vaults, on roughly 2.5m centres. The interior demonstrates contrasts between light and dark, wood, brick, painted stone walls and plywood panels. The drawings were handed over to an assortment of draughtsmen – Sakakura, Pollak, Streb, Miquel and others – for detailing (fig. 16).

It seems, suddenly, a long way away from Pierre's light-hearted adventures. Unfortunately, the first variants for the final scheme didn't take account of the position of the trees, which involved some drastic compression of the cellar stairs, kitchen and bathroom in the west wing.[30] The house as built classifies and orders its spaces, elevations and materials in a rigorous way. For all the bricolage and warmth of plywood, brick, grassed vaults and moellon surfaces, any trace of informality and the spirit of pioneering suburban living has vanished. The 'petite maison de week-end' carries the full burden of responsibility of the avant-garde villa. It is as though Pierre asked Le Corbusier whether he could build a cheerful, friendly, informal, socialist suburban dwelling, and Le Corbusier simply refused. But the suburb has had the last word.[31] The building has reverted to type, hiding behind its high hedge and fierce guard dog. It has sprouted Spanish grilles and a hideous extension, its stone flags and masonry now brightly picked out with coloured mortar.

NOTES

1. A. Fourcaut, *La Banlieue en Morceaux* (Paris, 2000), p. 224.
2. Ibid. p. 61.
3. For the communist deputy Beaugrand, the purpose of the Loi Loucheur was to 'vanquish the communist workers by turning them into house-owners' (debate in the Chambre des Députés 6 July 1928, *Journal Officiel, Debats Parlementaires* (1928), p. 2248). Only the communists voted against the Loi Loucheur. See also T. Benton, 'La réponse de Le Corbusier à la Loi Loucheur' in *Le Corbusier une Encyclopédie* (Paris, 1987), pp. 236–9.
4. F. Dubost, 'Le choix du pavillonnaire' in A. Faure (ed.), *Les Premiers Banlieusards* (Paris, 1991), p. 185 ff. The Communists voted for the Loi Sarraut, 9 March 1928, which delivered 8.4 million francs to sanitize estates predating the law of 1924. The Loi Sarraut helped to neutralize opposition in the *banlieue* by supporting some improvement while also forcing illegal settlers to become normalized by paying local taxes. (A. Fourcaut, op. cit. p. 198.)
5. See J.-C. Vigato, *L'Architecture Régionaliste* (Paris, 1994), C. Mauclair, *La Crise du Panbétonisme Intégrale: L'Architecture Va-t-Elle Mourir?* (Paris, 1933), G. Umbdenstock, *Cours d'Architecture de l'École Polytechnique, 1927* (Paris, 1930).
6. Annie Fourcaut observes that postwar research on the banlieue, such as it is, has

focused almost entirely on the social housing programmes in the *ceinture rouge*. '... the bourgeois suburbs remain *terra incognita*. No historical work on Saint Mandé or Enghien; hardly anything on rightwing suburban leaders such as Jean Goy or Senator Ernest Billiet...' A. Fourcaut, *Un Siècle de Banlieue Parisienne 1859–1964* (Paris, 1988), p. 20.
7. R. Haumont, in *L'Habitat Pavillonaire* (CRU, 1979), is not convinced of the political impact of house ownership; see his research as against H. R. Guerrand in *L'Histoire de la Vie Privée* (Paris, 1989), vol. 4, p. 380 ff.
8. B. Cendrars, *La Banlieue de Paris* (Paris, 1949; published in paperback 1966). For a provocative and fascinating comparison between Le Corbusier and Blaise Cendrars see J. Gubler, 'LC et BC: paragone difficile' in *Le Corbusier à Genève 1922–1932* (Lausanne, 1987), pp. 143–51.
9. B. Cendrars, op. cit. pp. 9–10.
10. Ibid. p. 19.
11. Ibid. pp. 36–7.
12. 'Madame G. from Coudreaux', in A. Faure (ed.), op. cit. p. 193.
13. Le Corbusier, *Une Maison un Palais* (Paris, 1928), p. 46.
14. The original sketches are in *Le Corbusier Sketchbooks*, vol. 1, pp. 389 and 390 (redrawn later and included in *The Radiant City*, p.29). The drawings were apparently labelled 'Toulouse Esbly', but there doesn't seem to be an Esbly near Toulouse. There is an Esbly, on the banks of the Marne, in the eastern suburbs of Paris, and it is to this that Le Corbusier probably refers.
15. T. Benton, 'La villa Mandrot i el lloc de la imaginacio', *Quaderns* 163, October–December 1984 and B. Reichlin, 'La Villa de Mandrot au Pradet (Var), 1929–34' in *Le Corbusier La Ricerca Patiente* (Lugano, 1980), pp. 87–96.
16. Le Corbusier, *La Ville Radieuse*, p. 91.
17. Ibid. p. 12.
18. Ibid. p. 38.
19. For example in 1892 A. Keufer feared that the appeal of house ownership would make the workers forget 'generous feelings' and lead them to lose 'the notion of their corporate duties' (A. Faure, op. cit. p. 176).
20. See F. Passanti, 'The Vernacular, Modernism and Le Corbusier', *Journal of the Society of Architectural Historians* 56:4, December 1997, pp. 438–51; J.-C. Vigato, 'Régionalisme' in *Le Corbusier une Encyclopédie* (Paris, 1987), pp. 56–7.
21. B. Reichlin, 'Cette belle pierre de Provence, La Villa de Mandrot', *Le Corbusier et la Mediterranée* (Marseilles, 1987), pp. 131–40.
22. Le Corbusier talks about 'my neighbour's wall' in a radio interview included on the CD-ROM published by the Fondation Le Corbusier.
23. The *devis descriptif* survives (FLC H2-19 123-130). The estimate comes to 40,500 francs.
24. H2 19 106, letter to Le Corbusier, 'chez monsieur Vidal au Piquey, Bassin d'Arcachon', 29 July 1935.
25. The diaries are notoriously difficult to use for checking dates, since they have few, if any, dates in them. Fortunately, the one for June 1934 to March 1935 gives up its secrets quite easily (FLC F3-5-9, p.53).
26. Le Corbusier, *Une Maison un Palais* (Paris, 1928), p. 46.
27. The drawing shows the dividing wall in the centre of the salon, in the penultimate phase of the project, just before 21 January 1935 (FLC 9295, 9254, 9245, 9257, 9242, 9243), before Pierre discovered that there was a tree in the way of the west extension of the house. The first two drawings for the final, reduced project (FLC 9255 and 24228) retain the stove, but all the other drawings introduce a fireplace on the east side of the divider.
28. On 13 January 1925 Henri Frugès wrote to Le Corbusier about the complaints of the first inhabitants of the sawmill cottages he had designed at Lege. 'People cannot understand a house without a hearth...they would love to have at least a fireplace and take pleasure in seeing a flickering fire...I must admit myself that, personally, I could never live in a house, however well heated it was, if I couldn't take pleasure in a roaring fire.' (FLC H1-17-131).
29. FLC F305, p. 356
30. e.g. FLC 9291, 9295, 9254, 9245, 9257, 9297, 9242, 9243, 9255, 9284.
31. See the student dissertation by C. Biehler, D. Fridez, D. May, M.-N. Schaaf, *La Maison de Le Corbusier à La-Celle-St-Cloud*, in the Fondation Le Corbusier library, which shows some recent photographs.

Fernando Pérez Oyarzun

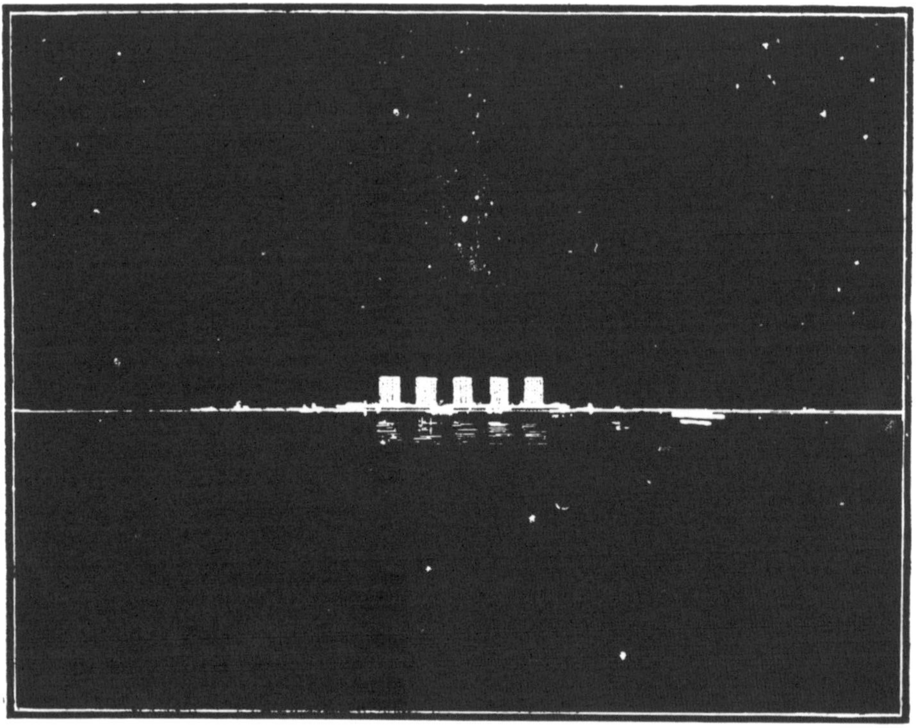

Le Corbusier in South America: Reinventing the South American City

The Traveller and the Swiss Contact

Precisions[1] was published by Le Corbusier in 1930 after his first visit to South America. It is a record of his state of mind in the wake of this journey. The title suggests a clarification and revision of his architectural ideas, which had become widely known but were the subject of controversy and misinterpretation. *Precisions* was published seven years after *Towards a New Architecture* and at a time when the first volume of his *Œuvre Complète* was about to appear.

Le Corbusier left Paris for South America at the end of September 1929 and returned in late December, having spent his forty-second birthday in Buenos Aires. His long lecture tour was intended both to win new commissions and to raise public awareness of modern architecture. As had been the case with his other travels, the stimulating atmosphere, and the encounters with new places and new people, provided him with the opportunity to make fresh discoveries and consequently to reconsider his aims and beliefs.

The book consists of twelve essays in total: ten given as lectures in Buenos Aires, one 'Brazilian Corollary' given as a lecture in Rio de Janeiro, and one 'American Prologue' written on the way home. In addition there are two appendices, 'The Temperature of Paris' and 'The Atmosphere of Moscow'. Towards the end of 'American Prologue', written on board the liner Lutetia on his way home, Le Corbusier recalls:

> It was at the home of the charming and so intelligent Duchess of Dato, in Paris, that I met Gonzalès Garraño. He urged me to go to Buenos Aires, to express the realities and the approaching destiny of modern architecture in that city in gigantic birth pangs. Besides, since 1925, Paulo Prado had been writing to me from São Paulo and Blaise Cendrars, in Paris, pushed me forward with arguments, geography maps and photographs.[3]

Besides putting Le Corbusier in touch with aristocrats and politicians, the traveller and writer Cendrars seems to have provided a more intimate background to the expedition. Cendrars, like Le Corbusier, was born in La Chaux-de-Fonds, Switzerland. Between 1924 and 1929 he visited South America five times, and as a result was well connected there, particularly

1. Le Corbusier, the five towers of the new Buenos Aires business district, seen from the river, *Precisions* image 305. 'In the waters of Rio I draw the lighted beacons, and in the Argentine sky the Southern Cross preceding millions of stars.'

among the intelligentsia of the Brazilian avant-garde. Many of these contacts – and in particular Paulo Prado – were also instrumental to Le Corbusier's visit. It is also clear that Le Corbusier and Cendrars were affected in similar ways by their respective travels in South America. The sequence of sketches in Le Corbusier's Sketchbook B4[4] – carefully registering the stations of his journey from France to South America – is reminiscent of 'Feuilles de Route',[5] written by Cendrars after his 1924 trip to South America. Cendrars' syncopated prose – a powerful mix of feelings, images and associations – or his almost objective and journalistic poetry, bear more than a passing resemblance to Le Corbusier's own writings and travel notes.[6] In a sense, one could see Le Corbusier's first South American journey as the architectural companion to Cendrars' poetic voyage.

This poetic tendency in Le Corbusier, which goes against the popular view of him as a pure rationalist, enjoyed an easy relationship with his complex, sometimes ambiguous attitude to both modern technology and European culture. During his South American journey he seems to have been less obsessed with the virtues of mechanical iconography and more focused on the natural environment, exotic human types, and the events of a supposedly epic conquest of the continent (figs. 2 & 3). That there was a significant shift in Le Corbusier's thinking around 1930 has been underlined by a number of critics, but it is not possible to attribute this shift to a single event, such as the South American journey. Instead, Colin Rowe's definition of Le Corbusier as an 'architectural dialectician',[7] offers a more complex interpretation of a mind that is in constant oscillation. Attracted by different poles of interest, rather than linear thinking processes, Le Corbusier frequently returned to topics for reinterpretation.

If we accept this theory, Le Corbusier's first South American experience should not be seen simply as a turning point in his evolution (although, at least in part, it was). Instead it marked the emergence of a new pole of reference for his discourse and architectural production. A newly acquired interest in nature and territory was soon reflected in his architecture and remained in his set of references and preferences, reappearing in alternative guises in his late projects.

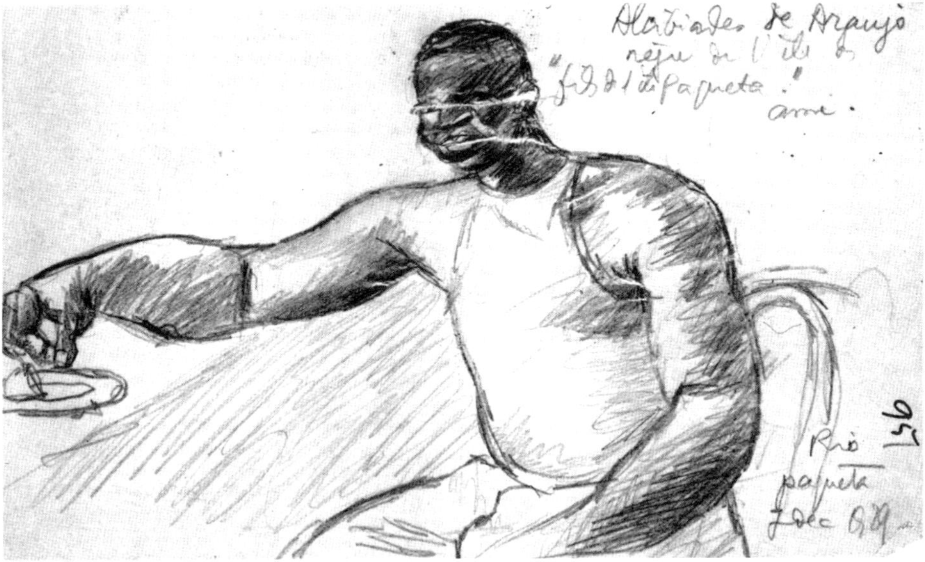

2. Le Corbusier, portrait of Alcibiades de Aranjo, Rio, 7 December 1929, no. 281 from Sketchbook B4, South America.

3. Le Corbusier, São Paulo, no. 260 from Sketchbook B4, South America.

Sketching From the Air

Le Corbusier's texts tend to avoid systematic development, being composed of independent, juxtaposed fragments which allow different readings. Descriptive sections alternate with reflections and memories, all of them intermittently summed up in short, punchy statements that recall a manifesto-style discourse. At once complex, synthetic and memorable, these statements can be seen as the basic units of his thinking.[8]

For Le Corbusier, sketches represented a similar kind of architectural aphorism, that was necessarily expressed iconographically. They had considerable value as devices of communication and even revelation. Related at once to architectural forms and thoughts, sketches were not the provisional traces of something waiting to be completed, but final products in themselves: snapshots that could not be finished or modified without losing their meaning. This is not far removed from Valéry's notion (expressed in relation to the work of Leonardo da Vinci),[9] that drawing can in itself be considered a way of thinking. Sketching was a significant component of the visit to South America, and Le Corbusier registered his feelings and impressions through a highly distinctive set of drawings, notable for their extensive use of colour, and for their emphasis on landscape and the human figure. Curiously, the drawings are rarely of buildings, and in most what would normally be understood as architecture appears as something acting almost by absence, suspended between the presence of territory and that of human bodies.

One of the most striking features of these South American sketches is the prominence of the aerial view. Aerial perspective also permeates the South American texts, as an expression of a new understanding of both territory and the city. Compared to Le Corbusier's previous references to aircraft,[10] there seems to have been a shift, from the conceptual and figuratively metaphoric paradigm of the airplane, towards the experiential and lyrical paradigm of flight (fig. 4).

It is said that Le Corbusier – who had so vividly expressed his admiration for aircraft – hadn't actually flown before his visit to South America. Whether or not this is true, the impact of the flight from Buenos Aires to Asunción del Paraguay over the Paraná river is evident in the texts and images included in *Precisions*. Previously held views seem to crystallize, while new ones emerge. A new scale, which Le Corbusier called 'territorial', was suddenly perceptible: the earth seen as a poached egg,[11]

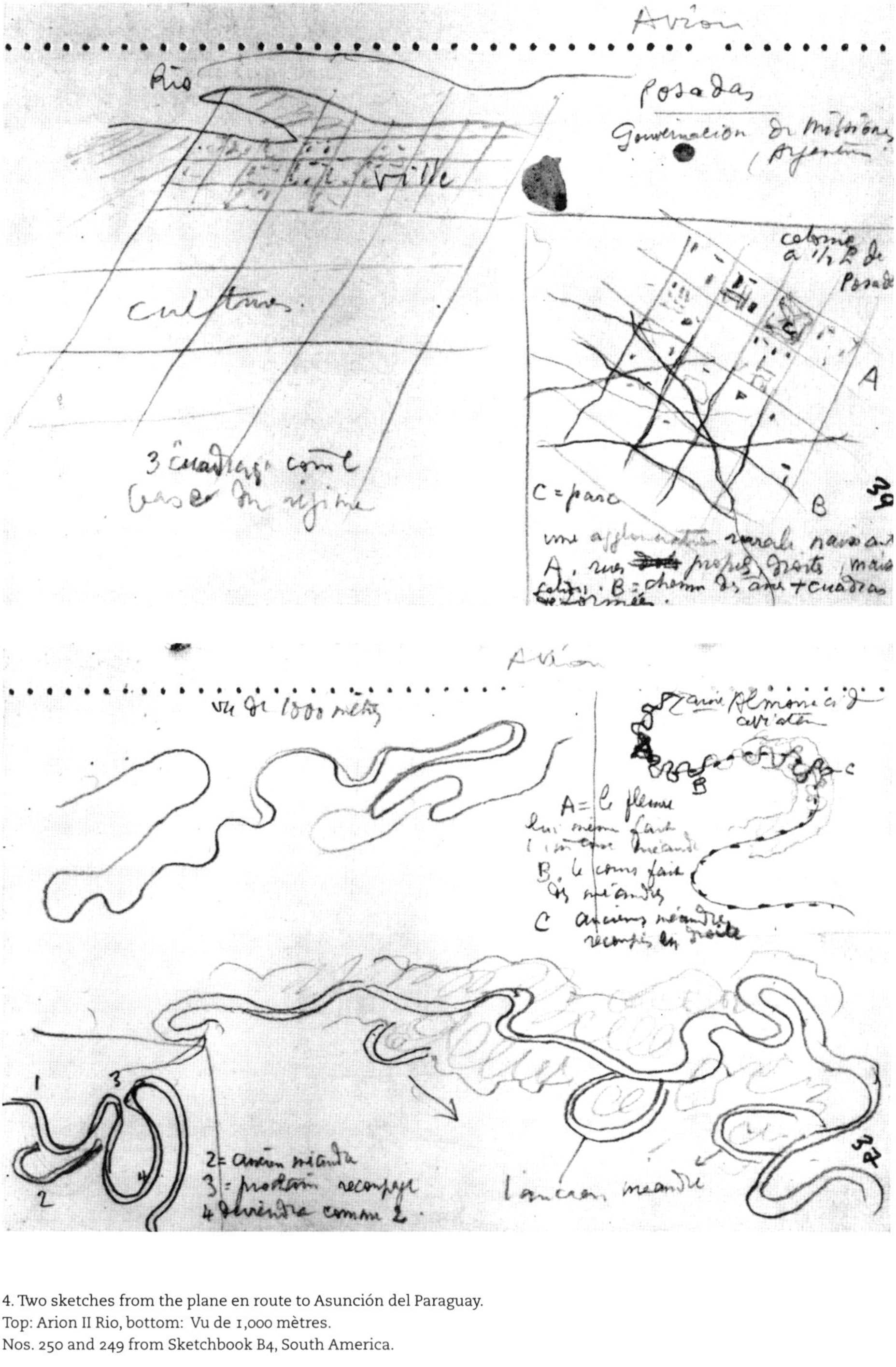

4. Two sketches from the plane en route to Asunción del Paraguay.
Top: Arion II Rio, bottom: Vu de 1,000 mètres.
Nos. 250 and 249 from Sketchbook B4, South America.

the cycles of the day, the symbolic power of the horizon and the established patterns of urban settlements. All of this appears in his discourse in a new, symphonic arrangement.

'At 500 to 1,000 metres altitude, and at 180 to 200 kilometres an hour', wrote Le Corbusier, 'the view from a plane is not rushed but slow, unbroken, the most precise that one can wish ... I exist in life only if I can see.'[12] Thanks to the airplane all became clear.[13] The 'law of the meander',[14] as he called it, emerged from his vision of the changing course of the river. It appears as a new geographical metaphor for the 'well-posed problem', in *Towards a New Architecture*.[15] This revelatory experience was vital to his understanding of the landscape and cities of South America.

Perhaps under the influence of Cendrars' poetic vision, the experience of flying also awakened the most lyric and telluric aspects of Le Corbusier's character. Nature – particularly nature seen from above – had a significant impact on his thoughts: 'from the plane I saw sights that one may call cosmic... those daring outlines of rocks that give us an idea of the sublime... if I think of architecture as the 'houses of man' I become Rousseauist...'.[16] From this aerial experience emerged a series of sketches, representing both the regular grid of South American settlements and the fluidity of the river courses: the near-Roman artificiality of the urban Spanish foundations and the monumental organic condition of the continent's geography. The polarity between city and nature seems to have been at the root of his South American urban proposals, which can be seen as the synthetic and propositional side of his analytical view from above. This is confirmed by both the references to aerial surveys in his urban proposals and his use of aerial perspective and the axonometric view in their representation.

Reinventing the South American City

Le Corbusier's first architectural responses to South America appear closely related to his previous work in Europe. A house for Victoria Ocampo, which had been commissioned in Paris before Le Corbusier's departure, seems to have been inspired by Maison Meyer or Villa Stein. Similarly, his first reaction to a local commission – a housing scheme in the surroundings of Buenos Aires – resembles a garden city made up of Villas Savoye, albeit with cypresses and palm-tree plantations.

Unlike those first attempts, the 1929 sketches for South American

5. 'From a plane, I draw an immense expressway for Rio', images 225 and 226 from Le Corbusier's *Precisions*.

cities – a kind of enthusiastic and inspired appendix to his Argentine and Brazilian lectures – reveal the torrent of new ideas that arose from his journey. Evolving over a period of just a few weeks, they seem to draw more on local experiences than his previous systematic and doctrinaire approach to urban problems. The sketch for Buenos Aires[17] (fig. 6) includes a business centre built on territory reclaimed from the river and symbolically dominated by an island airport. At first sight, the series of cruciform skyscrapers standing on a rectangular platform – with redents wings beyond them – appear to owe much to the Ville Contemporaine or the Plan Voisin. However, the section, showing the artificial extension of the downtown ground level over the Barranca gap, demonstrates a new attitude, deeply shaped by the physiognomy of the site. From another viewpoint, this sketch suggests an attempt to weave three elements into a single scheme: air (through the monumental placement of the airport), water (through the imposing presence of the river reopened towards the city) and earth (represented by the highway axis penetrating the city towards the pampa and the interior of the country). The classical five-tower facade (fig. 1) sums up the intentions of the project: a vertical and artificial statement set against the natural horizontality of the plain, under the openness of the Argentine sky.

Proposals for Montevideo and São Paulo (fig. 7) were drawn as axonometric views, suggesting that they had been conceived from above. Christened seascrapers[18] and earthscrapers[19] respectively, they were intended to explore the area between architecture and infrastructure, between building and city. Both schemes can be read as roads which become buildings, and as buildings conceived as large urban pieces. Territorial and horizontal traces build up a gesture against the irregularities of the coastal or meseta geography. Explicit references to Hadrian's Villa, the Segovia Aqueduct or the Pont du Gard indicate the sources of Le Corbusier's new urban attitude.

In Rio, similar principles were taken to an apotheosis of enthusiasm.[20] Linear city, elevated roads, monumental urban pilotis and, perhaps, the experience of the Lingotto[21] in Turin, are all arranged in a single flowing urban gesture. This has clearly been conceived from the air, in response to the exuberant but fragmented condition of the topography of the Guanabara bay. The Rio proposal, redeveloped in 1936, dreams of the possibility of enjoying the urban setting from 100 metres

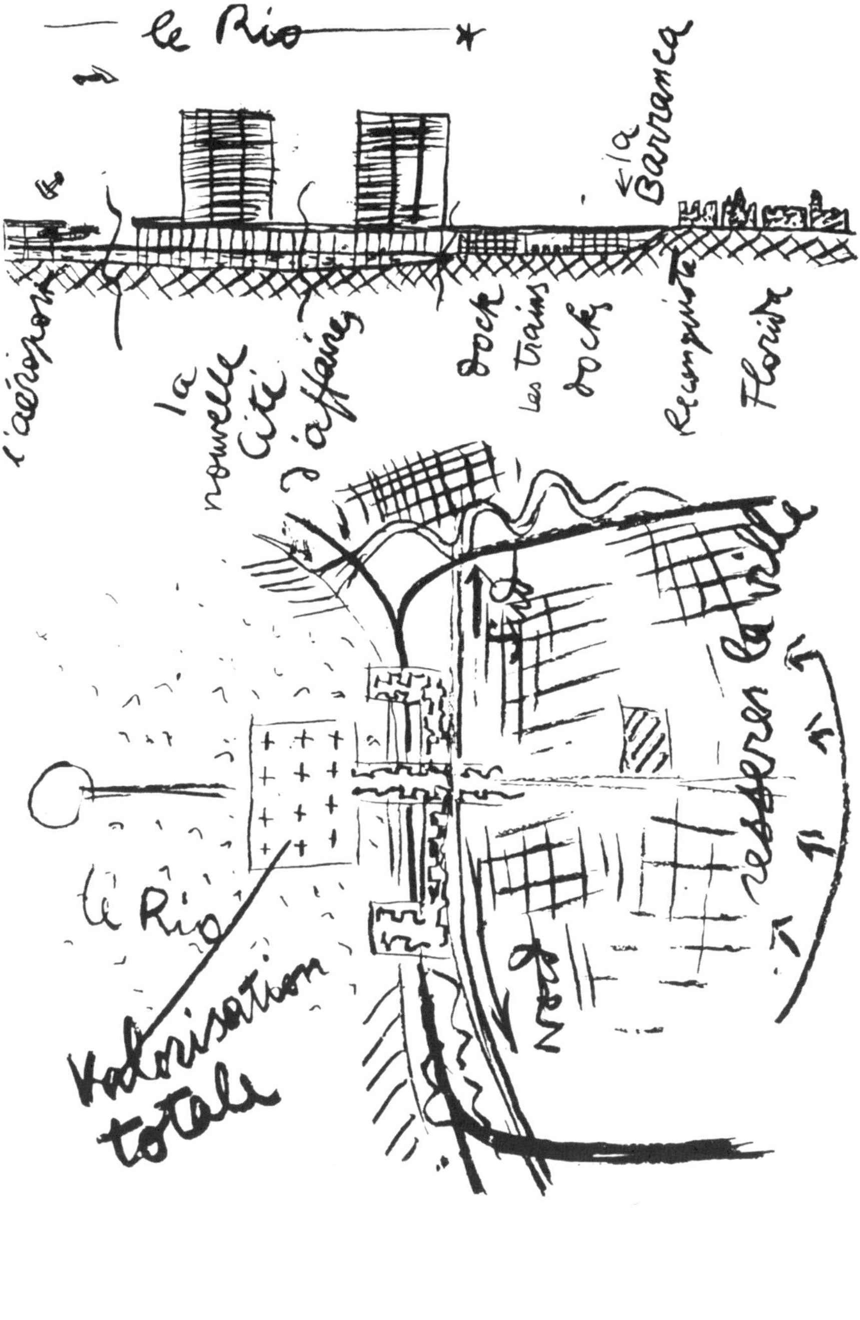

6. New business district, Buenos Aires, images 201 and 202 from *Precisions*.

in the air, and proposes a new mega facade for the city. Gigantic and threatening, this Brazilian megastructure signals a completely new approach whereby the modern city is superimposed upon the old city, creating an enormous urban collage.

Le Corbusier's career in South America, begun in 1929, is ultimately a catalogue of failures and misunderstandings. None of the Ministry of Health and Education, the University City for Rio de Janeiro (both in 1936); the plan for Buenos Aires (late 1930s and 1940s); the plan for Bogotá (1950s); and the French Embassy for Brasilia (1960s) were built. But nevertheless, Le Corbusier's experiences would later inform a series of projects for Algiers. There, a new version of the Buenos Aires towers, articulated with the Rio strip, created an urban ideogram superimposed onto both the existing city and its surrounding landscape. Ultimately, however, Algiers too was added to the list of Le Corbusier's urban failures.

Rather than Le Corbusier's huge urban proposals, it is two small houses, separated by almost 20 years, that epitomize his South American experience. The Errazuiz House (fig. 8), commissioned in Buenos Aires in 1929, though never built, was an important influence on Le Corbusier's work in the following years. Appearing as a revision of the Maison au Bord de la Mer of the early 1920s, it expresses, through rustic and traditional materials, Le Corbusier's response to the powerful geography of a remote and, for him, unknown site in Chile. The only project actually built by Le Corbusier in South America was the Currutchet House (fig. 9), completed in 1949. Reminiscent of the Cartago House, but enriched by the experience of the chorizo houses[22] he had sketched in Buenos Aires, it can be seen as a response to an ideal city, La Plata, which, in spite of being a product of the classical tradition attacked by Le Corbusier, is not so far removed from the grid pattern of his own Ville Contemporaine.

It is difficult to gauge what effect the journey to South America had on Le Corbusier: for all his experiences there, his later urban projects seem to return to doctrinaire urban principles rather than starting from empirical poetic suggestions. However, his spiralling mind never really visited the same place twice. The journey to South America allowed him to reconcile, at least momentarily, his faith in the spirit of a new age – represented by the experience of flight – with the myth of the primitive and the living traditions that he found in South American geography.

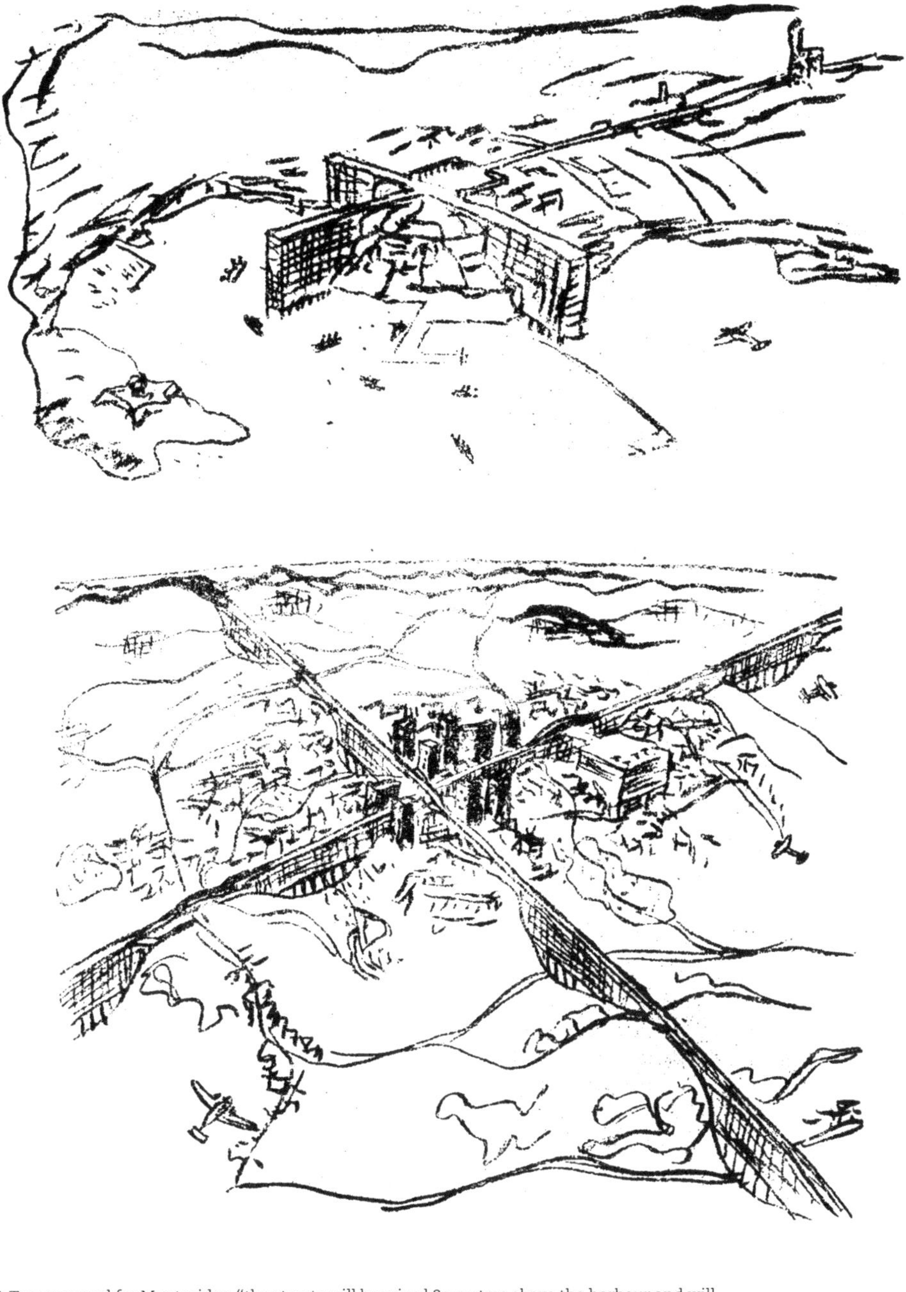

7. Top: proposal for Montevideo ('the streets will be raised 80 metres above the harbour and will stop abruptly in space'), bottom: proposal for São Paulo ('draw a horizontal of 45 kilometres from hill to hill, from summit to summit, then a second one at approximately right angles'). Images 223 and 224 from *Precisions*.

8. Le Corbusier, Errazuiz House, Zapallar, Chile, 1929–30, interior view, from *Œuvre Complète*.

9. Le Corbusier, Currutchet House, La Plata, Argentina, 1948–49.

NOTES

1. Le Corbusier, *Precisions on the Present State of Architecture and City Planning* (London, 1991). Originally published in French as *Précisions sur un État Présent de l'Architecture et de l'Urbanisme* (1930).
2. Le Corbusier, *Towards a New Architecture* (London, 1999). Originally published in French as *Vers une Architecture* (1923), English translation by John Rodker, 1927.
3. Le Corbusier, *Precisions*, op. cit. p. 18.
4. Le Corbusier, *Sketchbooks* (Paris, 1981). See vol. 1, 1914–1948, Sketchbook B4, which records his 1929 visit to South America.
5. B. Cendrars, 'Feuilles de Route' in *Œuvres Complètes*, vol. 1 (Paris, 1963), pp. 133–82. The first part, 'Le Formosa', which alludes to the name of the ship in which he travelled to South America, was published along with illustrations by the Brazilian painter Tarsilia do Amaral in 1924. The text's dedication is of interest: 'Ce cahier est dédié à mes bons amis de São Paulo Paulo PRADO, Mario Andrade, Serge Millet, Jasto de Almeida, Conto de Barros, Rubens de Mosaes, Luiz Aranhas, Oswaldo de Andrade, Yan et aux Amis de Rio de Janeiro Graza ARANHA, Sergia Buargne de Hollanda, Prudente de Moraes, Guillermo de Almeida, Ronald de Carvalho, Americo Faco, sans oublier l'inimitable et cher Léopold de FREITAS au Rio-Grande-do-Sul.' (*Œuvres*, p. 134, original spelling of the names).
6. There is a parallel between the emphasis that Le Corbusier places on his apartment on the Lutetia as a place of work in which he gave a final form to his lectures (Le Corbusier, *Precisions*, op. cit. p. 1) and Cendrars' description of himself in his apartment, surrounded by manuscripts and paper, in his poem 'Bagage' (included in 'Feuilles de Route', *Œuvres*, vol. 1, p. 149).
7. See C. Rowe, 'La Tourette' in *The Mathematics of the Ideal Villa and Other Essays* (London, 1976), p. 194.
8. This kind of aphoristic discourse is clearly seen in the introductory section of *Towards a New Architecture*, where brief paragraphs build up the argument.
9. In his well-known series of writings on Leonardo – *Introduction to the Method of Leonardo da Vinci* (1894), *Note and Digression* (1919) and *Leonardo and the Philosophers* (1929) – Valéry has examined the relationships between art and science and, in more general terms, between art and knowledge. In *Leonardo and the Philosophers*, referring to Leonardo, he states 'I mean that painting was his philosophy. The fact is that he said to himself, and he talked painting as others talk philosophy.' See P. Valéry, *Leonardo, Poe, Mallarmé* (London, 1972), p. 143.
10. Le Corbusier, *Towards a New Architecture*, op. cit. pp. 105–27.
11. Le Corbusier, *Precisions*, op. cit. pp. 5–6.
12. Ibid. p. 7.
13. Ibid. p. 235, '...when, by plane, everything has become clear, and you have learned this topography, this body so hilly and so complicated'.
14. Ibid. pp. 141–3. For Le Corbusier the meander is a metaphor for avoiding the real solution to modern urban problems, through minor attempts, until the moment at which a shortcut, in the form of a strong, avant-garde solution, allows the waters to flow straight again.
15. 'The lesson of the airplane is not primarily in the forms it has created, and above all we must learn to see in an airplane not a bird or a dragonfly, but a machine for flying; the lesson of the airplane lies in the logic which governed the enunciation of the problem and which led to its successful realization. When a problem is properly stated, in our epoch, it inevitably finds its solution.' Le Corbusier, *Towards a New Architecture*, op. cit. p. 110.
16. Le Corbusier, *Precisions*, op. cit. pp. 4, 5, 10.
17. Ibid. pp. 200–14.
18. Ibid. pp. 238–9.
19. Ibid. pp. 239–42.
20. Ibid. pp. 238–9.
21. Le Corbusier, *Towards a New Architecture*, op. cit. p. 287. The Fiat workshop at Turin with its rooftop testing track is illustrated in the book.
22. In spite of his attacks on the traditional urban block scheme, Le Corbusier expressed his admiration for some of the spontaneous constructions of Buenos Aires' old urban fabric. Chorizo (sausage) houses are developed in very deep, narrow sites. See Le Corbusier, *Precisions*, op. cit. pp. 211, 229.

Stanislaus von Moos

1. Types of urban agglomerations: Pera, Istanbul, Rome and Siena, illustration from *L'Esprit Nouveau* 21, 1924.

2. The architect as buffoon: the closing party of the first CIAM congress at La Sarraz, 1928 (Le Corbusier is fourth from the left).

Architecture and Grand Tourism

I

Le Corbusier's conception of what he called the 'Synthesis of the Arts' is often explained in terms of morphological analogies: a purist still-life and a floor plan of the Villa Savoye placed side by side; the meandering outlines of those voluminous female nudes of the 1930s and 1940s set next to the Plan Obus for Algiers (1931). Perhaps more complex constellations need to be evoked if one wishes to study Le Corbusier's relationship with the visual arts from a standpoint that is not exclusively architectural, but that incorporates a broader view of the cultural history of the visual arts.

A clue to this approach is offered by the curious group – or strip – of rapidly executed sketches that refer to places that Le Corbusier (or rather Charles-Édouard Jeanneret, as he was known at the time) visited during his Grand Tour (fig. 1). This strip – a casual reflection of the well-known paintings that depict the collections of famous eighteenth-century Grand Tourists (fig. 3) – serves as an illustration to an article entitled 'Classement et Choix' ('Ordering and Choice') that appeared in issue 21 of *L'Esprit Nouveau*. An inventory of emblematic city-types (or so it appears), the strip includes a drawing of Pera, a suburb of Istanbul – where Le Corbusier and Klipstein had rented a room in 1911 – and, immediately below, a view of Istanbul from the Bosporus. Then follows a catalogue of geometric forms (cube, cylinder, pyramid) symbolizing Rome, and finally, at the bottom, a drawing made after a seventeenth-century print that shows the 'skyline' of Siena. (It is no coincidence that this skyline also reminds one of New York, a recurring theme in *L'Esprit Nouveau* from the very beginning.)

In order to make this illustration, or sequence of illustrations, look like a systematic demonstration that might function as a basis for 'Ordering and Choice', notes have been added in the margins – it is unfortunate that you have to twist your neck in order to read them. Those postulate a correspondence between the images and the 'character' of the places they represent:

> *Pera:* the saw-blade of the city of merchants, pirates, gold-seekers.
>
> *Stet:* the ardour of the minarets, the calmness of the flattened domes. Allah vigilant but orientally imperishable.
>
> *Rome:* geometry, the implacable order, war, civilization, organization.

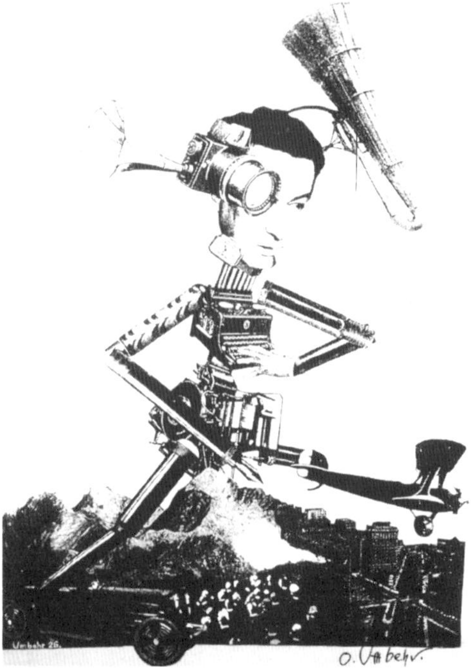

3. Giovanni Paolo Panini, *Views of Ancient Rome with the Artist Finishing a Copy of the Adolbrandini Wedding ('Roma Antica')*, 1755.

4. Umbo, *Der rasende Reporter* (The Speeding Reporter), photomontage portrait of Erwin Egon Kisch, 1926.

> *Siena*: the anguished tumult of the Middle Ages. Hell and paradise (anticipating the 1935 view of New York as '*belle et digne catastrophe*').

When it comes to the question of what sense should be made, ultimately, of this 'menu' and its display of 'diversity' ('*la diversité d'un menu bien fait*', as Le Corbusier says in a comment on this illustration) one is left with a riddle: is diversity among these urban forms actually the issue? I don't think so. Rather than architectural typologies we are dealing with a typology of visual means that represent cityscapes in graphic terms: first (at the top of the page) the rapid 'impression' of the urban skyline integrated in the landscape; then (in the middle) the typological inventory of the monumental architecture of Rome, and finally (at the bottom) the quotation of a historic *veduta*.

The image also begs another series of questions: why associate 'impression' with Pera or Istanbul? Why the typological inventory with Rome? And why the antiquarian *veduta* with Siena? Why should not Istanbul instead of Rome be subjected to a typological 'scanning'? And why should Rome not be represented as a classical landscape in the tradition of Corot or Ingres (two painters who were extraordinarily present in *L'Esprit Nouveau*)? The illustration offers no answers. Clearly, these associations primarily reflect biographical coincidence. We can safely say that the focus of interest lies not so much in the facts of the four cities and their physical forms); instead it has shifted towards the mechanism of their perception. And thus the seemingly arbitrary listing of the 'menu', this rudimentary '*Bilderatlas*' that is never systematically followed up, makes no sense in terms of architectural – let alone urban – theory. Unless, of course, we see it as something between a late variation on the theme of the '*voyage pittoresque*', common among architects of the late eighteenth and early nineteenth centuries, and a montage of visual headlines comparable to those used by journalists (since the crude visual shorthand of rapid sketches and the short, hardly readable, captions are devised as if in order to be compatible with the condition of speed under which such imagery is consumed as well as produced). It is not extravagant here to think of Egon Kisch, the 'Speeding Reporter', as represented in an almost contemporary collage by Umbo (1926) (fig. 4). Kisch was a German author who practised the journalistic travel report as a literary genre – as indeed did Le Corbusier himself, as I will argue later on.

5. 'Mr Pencil examining his work', from Rodolphe Toepffer's *Histoire de Mr Pencil*, 1840.

6. Childhood photograph, before 1900, of Charles-Édouard Jeanneret (right) with his brother Albert (second from left) and their cousins.

As for the '*voyage pittoresque*', one may turn to the work of Rodolphe Toepffer, a nineteenth-century Swiss pedagogue and illustrator, that might be seen as a forerunner of the 'comic strip'. In an album of 1840 illustrating *L'Histoire de Mr Pencil* (the name speaks for itself), Toepffer describes the mores of an English tourist on his way to discover Switzerland (as well as himself) with the help of 'pencil' studies of the visited sites. On the first page of the book, Mr Pencil, '*qui est artiste*', is seen initially in his role as an observer of nature and then as a connoisseur of art, contemplating the artistic quality of his work from various angles – including upside down (fig. 5). I like to think that this album is at the centre of a charming early photograph of the Jeanneret family (fig. 6). In any case, it is very likely that the family owned the book.

II

It is difficult not to be both charmed and somewhat confused by the eclecticism of the studies Le Corbusier – a Mr Pencil in the lingering tradition of the Grand Tour – made during the years of his itinerant education in Italy, Germany, Turkey and Greece. Depending on time, place and circumstance, he either adopts the gaze of the 'specialist' or that of the 'tourist'. The entire spectrum of the lessons taken in La Chaux-de-Fonds is eagerly displayed, first of all in the many letters sent to his parents, his friends and the '*Lieber Meister*', Charles L'Éplattenier. Paintings seen in museums and churches are examined alternatively as decorative surface organization – with Owen Jones in mind – or in the light of the aura that has been handed down by the official narratives of art history. At other times, the focus is shifted to colouring.

As to architecture, quality is either a question of principle – i.e. a matter of prejudice in favour of an international Gothic (not surprising in the light of his first built project) at the expense of Giotto and Brunelleschi – or a matter of the chromatic effects produced by the reflection of a sunset on a building. An example is the letter, dated 19 September 1907, that describes a visit to Pisa:

> At six o'clock, the cathedral is a chromatic enchantment, it is the quintessence of all variations of yellow, of ivory-white and black patina on an extraordinary ultramarine; as one continues to look at it, it becomes completely black. The part on which the baptistery casts its shadow vibrates softly in rich, yellow

> nuances; there is inlaid red marble, about to awake, and black marble turning blue; it is the revenge of the flat surfaces, they vibrate and speak softly. At 7 o'clock in the evening, the cathedral is even more beautiful than ever before (...)
> Behind me the sky is orange and mallow, the green of the doors has died, and yellow marble emerges (etc.)...

Then comes this reference to the complementary colour contrast (ever since Delacroix and Seurat a fundamental theme in avant-garde art):

> Some *bambini* are playing in the foreground, one of them with a scarlet dress in front of one of the green bronze doors.

Just a few days later, in Siena, Le Corbusier, working as a painter, attempted to capture the chromatic effects he had previously described in words (fig. 7). Although the motif is architectural – Siena's medieval Palazzo Pubblico – the title of this work is *Après L'Orage* ('After the Storm'), and what is depicted is the light effect in the aftermath of a thunderstorm. A green cloud is set off against the red facade of the town hall, a purple patch of sky that answers the yellow cap of the campanile – these colours are evidently not copied from nature. They are 'not of a descriptive, but of an evocative character; by all means symbolic', as Le Corbusier wrote at the same time in some other context. Most intriguingly, after having completed this quasi-Nabis watercolour, he went on to produce an industriously compiled study of the Baptistery facade that was only minutes away – radically changing registers and returning to the Ruskinian mode of depiction (fig. 8). Ruskin of course was the overriding ideological influence during Le Corbusier's trip to Italy, and in terms of this influence Le Corbusier's record of the interior view of S. Croce in Florence is probably among the more interesting documents (fig. 9). In his notes on the drawing Le Corbusier implicitly contradicts Ruskin, as he insists on the beauty of the simple roof (Ruskin, in *Mornings in Florence* denounces the interior for its lack of vaulting). In other notes, Le Corbusier comments on proportion and the effects of light – a subject he appears to have discussed thoroughly with his travel companion Léon Perrin, since Perrin's own drawing, clearly executed from exactly the same spot, is all about light (fig. 10). Needless to say, this genre or type of the annotated sketch was the one most often used in subsequent decades by Le Corbusier the 'traveller' or the '*touriste impénitant*', as he described himself.

The recent exhibition I curated with Arthur Rüegg – and the cata-

7. Le Corbusier, *Après l'Orage*, study of Palazzo Pubblico, Siena, 1907.

8. Le Corbusier, facade and details of Baptistery, Siena, 1907.

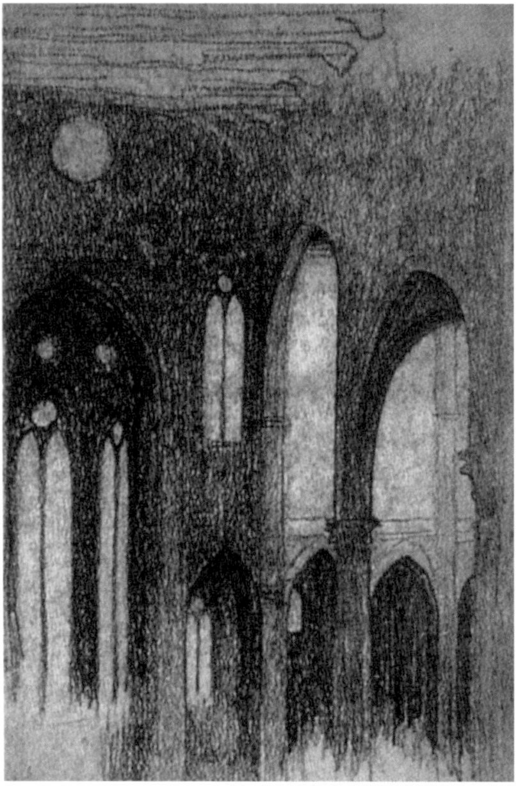

9. Le Corbusier, interior study of S. Croce, Florence, 1907.

10. Léon Perrin, interior view of S. Croce, Florence, 1907.

logue that goes along with it (*Le Corbusier before Le Corbusier*, 2002/2003) – give a number of examples that illustrate Le Corbusier's extremely eclectic way of building up a personal archive of references from which to work, especially as he moves from his early guise as a diligent student at the local art school to an architect who has come of age and who also practises the 'fine arts' (i.e. from making architectural studies in the tradition of Ruskin or, a little later, Schultze-Naumburg, to producing things that make more explicit claims to being taken seriously as 'art'). I have tried to argue elsewhere that Le Corbusier's vision of Istanbul (or that part of his vision articulated in the 'art' – as opposed to 'architecture' – register) is a tribute to neo-Impressionism, or at least an exercise in neo-Impressionism, and more precisely a tribute to Paul Signac. In fact, in a letter to Ritter, Le Corbusier speaks at length about a painting by Signac he had seen in Munich and that shaped his ideas about what to expect in Istanbul.

III

What sense is to be made of this potentially annoying 'diversity' or apparent lack of coherence in the work? Here I am referring not only to Le Corbusier before Le Corbusier (i.e. before he changed his name), but to the entire arc of his *Œuvres Complètes* and the mixed bag of architecture, painting, sculpture, photography it contains – including, of course, the admonition that an architect should never use a camera…). Is this to be attributed to a particularly developed capacity for carnivalesque disguise? In fact we have many pictures that show the architect in clown-like postures (fig. 2) but we should also remember that as an editor of *L'Esprit Nouveau*, Le Corbusier was using some four to five *noms de plume* at the same time. Or should one concede that art is a 'biological' fatality that finds its explanation in itself and thus that we should be content in understanding it (and perhaps life) as the simple acting out of the lessons one has learned in one's school days? And should one accept that this acting out, this surfing on waves of art in order always to remain on top of events, will be all the more breathtaking if those lessons were taken from life rather than from books?

Moreover, should we see in the architect's efforts to prevent any conception of him as a simply competent professional (and worse, a mere 'specialist') a '*touche à tout*', an all-rounder who will do just about anything as the reprise of a classical ideal of human fulfilment? (A conception that postulates that man is only a man if he is capable of acting out the spectrum of capacities for which his body and his mind have made him fit.) If such is the case, then the very idea of the Grand Tour appears as a key to at least some of the riddles that this work represents. For the Grand Tour is both an institution and a model of learning, perhaps, even, a way of life – as it has been brought to our attention, in recent years, by the work of Attilo Brilli, Cesare de Seta and others (cf. fig. 1).

It is worth remembering that the *carte d'identité*, which was issued at around 1940 to the name 'Le Corbusier' identified him as 'homme de lettres' – at a time when even a customs officer may have recognized him as an internationally renowned architect. Oscillating between the roles of storyteller and theoretician, moralist and technician, exploiting a multitude of voices from intimate raconteur to forensic preacher, Le Corbusier often used his travels as a springboard for his didactic and doctrinal discourse. Most of his early points of reference in some way belong to the genre of the travel account – writings by Hippolyte Taine (*Voyage en Italie*), William Ritter (*L'Entêtement Slovaque*), Théophile Gautier and many others (including, by the way, Montaigne and even Homer. Indeed his work as a writer was literally bracketed by the theme of travel, from the articles written for the *Feuille d'Avis* in La Chaux-de-Fonds in 1911 to the *Voyage d'Orient* prepared in 1965, in the last months of his life.

The theme also left its mark on most of the books that appeared inbetween, in subtitles such as 'Voyage au Pays des Timides' (fig. 11), becoming an almost annoying pose. *Précisions* (1930), a collection of ten lectures delivered in Argentina and Brazil, is an interesting example. The dynamite of its introduction ('Prologue Américain') and visionary post-script ('Corollaire Brésilien') is far more powerful than the declamatory and repetitive rhetoric of the lectures themselves. The beginning emphasizes the authenticity of the experience – and of course, the ocean liner is part of the spectacle described in the book (it had already been insistently present in *Vers une Architecture* (fig. 12)):

> 10 december 1929
> on board the *Lutetia*
> along the coast of Bahia.
> The Compagnie Sud-Atlantique has kindly put at my disposal
> a luxury apartment, and thus, far from the noise of the engine

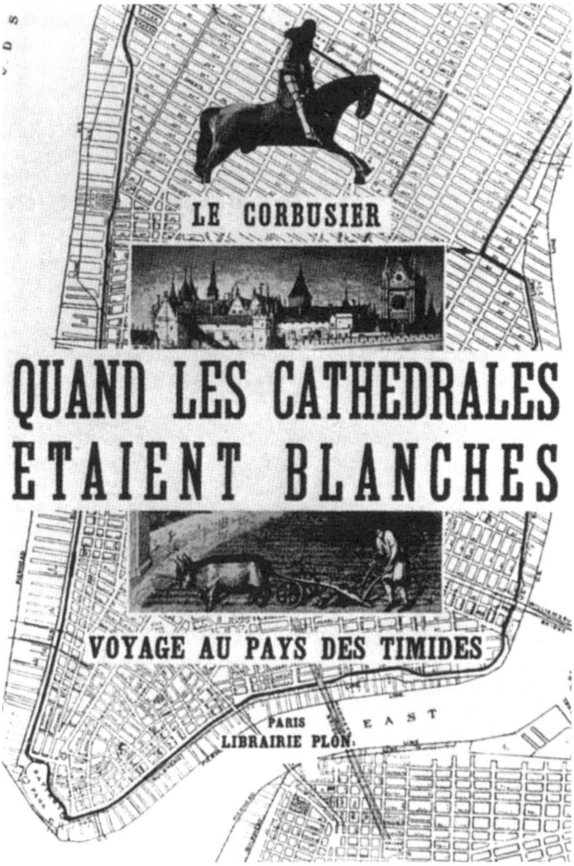

11. *Quand les Cathédrales Étaient Blanches. Voyage au Pays des Timides*, Paris, 1936, book jacket designed by Le Corbusier.

12. 'Compagnie Générale Transatlantique', advertisement designed by Le Corbusier or Amédée Ozenfant and published in *L'Esprit Nouveau* 8, 1921.

celle-ci contraste d'autant plus avec le milieu naturel que son but est plus près de la pensée et plus éloigné, plus détaché du corps. On peut dire que plus les œuvres humaines s'éloignent de la préhension directe, plus elles tendent à la pure géométrie : un violon, une chaise qui touchent notre corps sont d'une géométrie amoindrie, mais la ville est de pure géométrie. Libre, l'homme tend à la pure géométrie. Il fait alors ce qu'on appelle de l'ordre.

L'ordre lui est indispensable, sinon ses actes seraient sans cohésion, sans suite possible. Il y ajoute, y apporte, l'idée d'excellence. Plus l'ordre est parfait, plus il est à l'aise, en sécurité. Il échafaude dans son esprit des constructions basées sur cet ordre qui lui est imposé par son corps, et il crée. L'œuvre humaine

13. Title page from Rodolphe Toepffer's *Voyages en Zigzag*, Paris, 1846.

14. Switchbacks in San Francisco and on an Alpine pass.
Page from Le Corbusier, *Urbanisme*, Paris, 1925.

and on the most quiet spot of the ship I can tackle the final editing of my ten lectures.

And the climax is reached, of course, in the concluding pages of the book, where the architect proposes for Rio a building that would be simultaneously a freeway and a horizontal 'skyscraper': a wonderful, colossal and impossible building in which tourism and urbanism have become one.

IV

Decades ago (it must have been in the spring of 1968), Albert Jeanneret told me that his younger brother Charles-Édouard (Le Corbusier) made his earliest drawings as copies after Rodolphe Toepffer's *Voyages en Zigzag*. I had not heard of the book before and so the information was never acted upon. More recently, both terms – 'voyages' and 'zigzag' – began to exert a strange fascination (fig. 13). Not only because of the many variations on the 'zigzag' theme in Le Corbusier's later urbanistic textbooks: from the famous 'donkey's path' of Sittean origin to the meandering rivers of South America in *Précisions*, including of course the very switchbacks on Alpine passes that Toepffer had on his title page and of which Le Corbusier gives a modern version in *Urbanisme*, 1925 (fig. 14). As illustrator, Toepffer (who lived from 1799 to 1846) was a contemporary of Gustave Doré and Grandville, yet at the same time, as head of a private boarding school in Geneva, he could be seen together with Jean-Jacques Rousseau (whom he admired) and Heinrich Pestalozzi as part of an enlightened triumvirate of men engaged in the reform of education. *Voyages en Zigzag* is a rare document in the early history of tourism. It eloquently illustrates its origins in educational reform on the one hand, and its role in the commodification of the picturesque landscape on the other. In fact some of the illustrations in the book are by Alexandre Calame, the Swiss painter of romantic Alpine scenes .

Early on (in a letter to Auguste Klipstein), Le Corbusier confessed that he 'would be delighted to write a doctoral thesis' on Toepffer. That his enthusiasm survived into the 1920s is confirmed by a seven-page 'strip' by Toepffer published in *L'Esprit Nouveau*, a 'strip' that was made of sections taken from *L'Histoire du Dr Festus* and *L'Histoire de Mr Pencil*, and that was accompanied by a short article signed 'de Fayet', a pseudonym used by both editors, under the title 'Toepffer Précurseur du Cinéma'

15. Rodolphe Toepffer, *L'Histoire de Mr Pencil*, Paris, 1840, extract published in *L'Esprit Nouveau* 11/12, 1921, 'Les vignettes se succèdent comme les feuillets de petits cinés en carnet...'

16. Plate 24 from Le Corbusier, 50 *Aquarelles de Music-Hall ou le 'QUAND-MÊME' des Illusions*, 1926.

(fig. 15). Which is to say that Toepffer's 'comic strip' interested *L'Esprit Nouveau* not as a mere souvenir of the culture of the Grand Tour (as mediated in a children's book from an era that belonged to Le Corbusier's grandparents), but as an anticipation of modern cinema. In fact the caption in *L'Esprit Nouveau* says:

The vignettes follow each other like little movies in book form.

Somewhat later, in 1926, Le Corbusier produced a number of watercolours on the theme of the Music Hall – obviously relating to Toepffer – and gave them to Levaillant, with the following caveat:

> I am enclosing with the bundle some instructions for use. No kidding! These daubs are not to be framed. It only works when seen rapidly, cinematically. I rely on you... (fig. 16)

V

There are many proofs for Le Corbusier's fascination with film. Sergei Eisenstein, no less, quoted the architect as having referred to cinema as the key medium of the modern era. What is interesting with regard to Toepffer in this context is that, seen from the 1920s, he appears to bridge the spheres of tourism and cinema as two emblematic cultural realities in the no-man's land between art and mass culture. By 1910, and with artists like Robert Delaunay or Fernand Léger, this no-man's land had become a favoured hunting ground for the Parisian avant-garde. Symbolism, Unanimism, and Futurism had shown the way. Not to mention the novelist and poet Blaise Cendrars, alias Freddy Sauser, born in La Chaux-de-Fonds, in 1887 – the same year as Le Corbusier (they later met and became friends). Cendrars can be said to have inaugurated a specifically avant-garde tradition of the travel account, based (among others), on Filippo Marinetti's *Parole in Libertà*, while also referring explicitly to the techniques of the screenplay.

The Grand Tour, though still enacted by some as an ancestral rite – as in the case of Jeanneret/Le Corbusier's and Klipstein's touchingly old-fashioned *Voyage d'Orient* in 1911 – had in the meantime changed both its technology and its ethos. Railways and World Fairs had made topical aspects of the Grand Tour into a commodity and it is this aspect that began to interest the avant-garde. Among many comparable events at the Paris World's Fair of 1900 was a 'train' that offered a voyage of the entire Trans-Siberian Railway that could be experienced without leaving the Fair. This was achieved not with the help of cinema, but with the use of a moving panorama. I mention this exhibit because it served as an inspiration for the famous *Prose du Transsibérien et de la Petite Jehanne de France* (1913), a 'simultaneous poem' made of words and images by Cendrars and the painter Sonia Delaunay. Perhaps this precious *leporello* is the founding moment in the artistic conceptualization of modern travelling, based as it is on the railway map of Russia overlaid by a virtual geography of places Cendrars appears to dream of while on his fictional voyage (fig. 19).

Although this leaves the argument somewhat open-ended, I believe that a case can be made for a discussion of modern architecture in terms of its interrelatedness both with the Grand Tour *and* with cinema. And in the context of such a discussion Toepffer, and perhaps even the jigsaw-line of the switchbacks on his title page – mirrored in Sonia Delaunay's spiralling puffs of colour – might occupy a central position. Le Corbusier was notoriously slow in absorbing the impact of the avant-garde – the *Prose du Transsibérien* would have appeared esoteric if not nonsensical to him, had he known it around 1913, when it was created. But when he did absorb the impact of the avant-garde, albeit belatedly, he often managed to produce images that would sum it all up.

A page from *La Ville Radieuse*, 1934, illustrating the elaborate traffic system of Venice, is at once thematically close and stylistically remote from the world of the avant-garde. Of course, it is basically no more than a travel brochure (fig. 17), yet the curve of the Grand Canal curiously recalls the meanders sketched in *Précisions* that I have referred to earlier. It is highlighted not only as the traffic route for the *vaporetti*, but as a curving form, as found in nature (and in medieval urbanism) and analogous to the switchbacks on an Alpine pass in Switzerland, it suggests that it is the very bending of the curve that allows for the perception, in rapid sequence, of a series of images that are displayed in a 'cinematographic' fashion along the two edges. It is almost 'a movie in book form', to use Le Corbusier's own expression (although one would certainly not describe it as a 'typographical movie-spectacle' ('*typografische Kinoschau*'), as Lissitzky had described one of his own exhibition designs some years previously.

Seen in such a way (if you allow me, too, to be really sketchy), the curve, spiralling up like a ramp or a system of stairs within a house – as

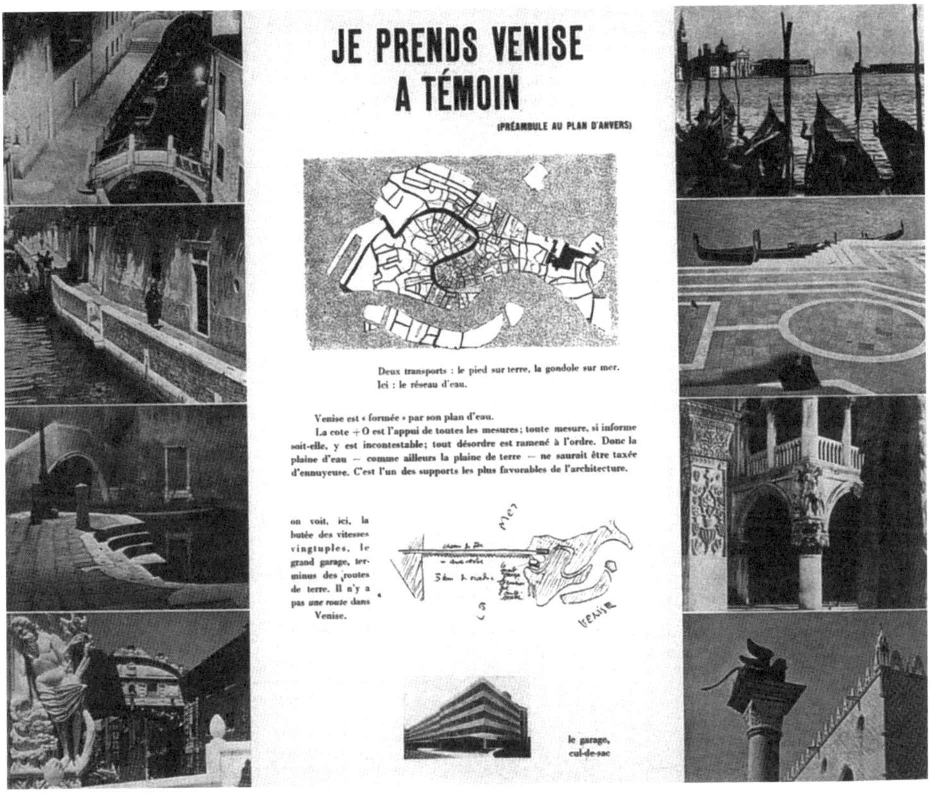

JE PRENDS VENISE A TÉMOIN

(PRÉAMBULE AU PLAN D'ANVERS)

Deux transports : le pied sur terre, la gondole sur mer.
Ici : le réseau d'eau.

Venise est « formée » par son plan d'eau.

La cote +O est l'appui de toutes les mesures; toute mesure, si informe soit-elle, y est incontestable; tout désordre est ramené à l'ordre. Donc la plaine d'eau — comme ailleurs la plaine de terre — ne saurait être taxée d'ennuyeuse. C'est l'un des supports les plus favorables de l'architecture.

on voit, ici, la butée des vitesses vingtuples, le grand garage, terminus des routes de terre. Il n'y a pas *une route* dans Venise.

le garage, cul-de-sac

17. 'Je prends Venise à témoin', from Le Corbusier, *La Ville Radieuse*, 1935.

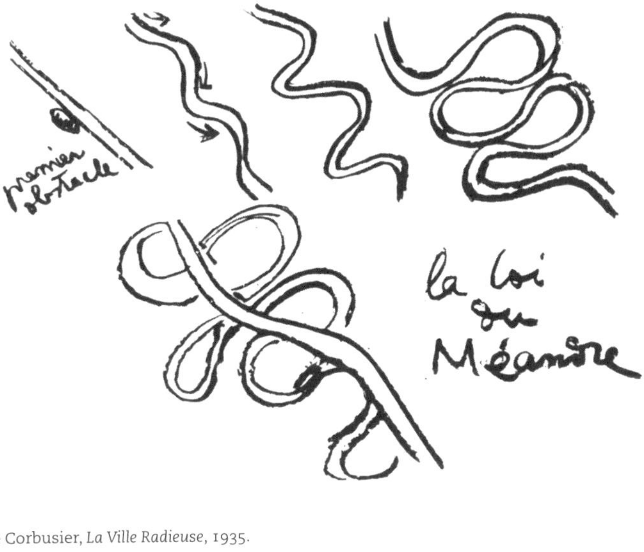

18. 'La loi du méandre', from Le Corbusier, *Précisions*, 1930.

19. Sonia Delaunay and Blaise Cendrars, *Prose du Transsibérien et de la Petite Jehanne de France*. leporello, Paris, 1913. The left strip shows Delaunay's colour composition alone, the right strip as it was printed in combination with the text.

20. Le Corbusier, Villa La Roche–Jeanneret, Paris, 1923–5, view of the entrance hall as envisioned in July 1923.

is described, for example, in a beautiful rendering illustrating an early project for the Villa La Roche in Paris – has the function not only to allow for circulation, but also to make circulation into an experience that deserves to be called a 'promenade' (fig. 20). A memory of Toepffer is somehow combined with a tribute to Rousseau (I am referring to the latter's *Promenades Solitaires*; and it is worth remembering that it is with respect to the Villa La Roche that Le Corbusier first used the term 'promenade architecturale'). We know that, for reasons that don't need to be discussed here, in the final project the movement of the promenade through the hall – was arrested and translated into a crystalline composition of rectangular surfaces and volumes which, compared to the earlier version, appears like a still. Later, however, the interrelated themes of spiral, switchback and cinema are developed further – in the Villa Savoye: with the spiral stair encased in the building box and the 'zigzag' ramp artfully devised as an instrument that can allow for a dynamic 'Vision in Motion' – as in a post-Cubist panopticon.

VI

I conclude with an all-too famous passage from the philosopher Ernst Bloch's *Das Prinzip Hoffnung* ('The Principle of Hope'), a passage which may or may not make sense in connection with this image of the roof of the Unité d'Habitation in Marseilles (fig. 22). Modern houses look as if they were 'ready to go', Bloch says, like 'boxes on mobile stilts', if not like boats. They have 'flat decks, bull's eyes, metal stairs, deck rails. They are glowing white (...). As boats, they would like to disappear.' My resorting to Bloch was perhaps inevitable here, if only because, once again, and from a totally different point of view, modern architecture is described in terms of travelling, an imagery of tourism that is evoked by its forms. I don't need to insist that for Bloch this machine imagery was synonymous both with a radical rejection of historic reference, and with a tragic failure to produce 'home'.

> For more than a generation, therefore, this steel-furniture, concrete-cube and flat-roof-obsession has been with us, extremely modern and boring, apparently bold but essentially trivial, full of hatred against the alleged superfluousness of any ornament, and more slavishly stuck in dogmatism than any copying after historic styles in the ominous nineteenth century.

21. Le Corbusier, drawing and written notes on a paperback edition of Homer's *Iliad* (1953 edition). The drawing by John Flaxman, copied (below) in summary fashion by Le Corbusier, shows the dead body of Sarpedon, the son of Zeus, carried by Sleep and Death towards Lykia, Sarpedon's native province. Notes refer to Le Corbusier's own return to Paris on 30 April 1961 from New York, where he had received a Gold Medal and Honorary Doctorate.

22. Le Corbusier, Unité d'Habitation, Marseilles, 1947–52, roof terrace.

Since these lines were written, Le Corbusier's architecture has itself evolved and changed, as is demonstrated by the Unité d'Habitation, a building that has frequently been descibed as a large ocean liner stranded on the coast of Marseilles (fig. 22). But it also has been described, with equal justification, as an evocation of the Athenian Acropolis. The theme of the boat is reiterated on the roof terrace, where it is recast as an archaic icon: the gymnasium roof clearly recalls a ship turned upside down and cut at both ends. Perhaps it is the ruin of the ship of the Argonauts – if not of the boat on which Ulysses crossed the Hersperides before he returned to Ithaca.

Taking into account Le Corbusier's interest, especially during the last years of his life, in Homer's *Iliad* and *Odyssey*, the archetypal travel account of western civilization, then this interpretation is by no means as extravagant as it at first seems (fig. 21). In the light of these discussions, one may wonder if Bloch's diatribe against the 'flat decks, bull's eyes, metal stairs, deck rails' in modern architecture, should be restricted to its explicitly stylistic implications rather than taken seriously on a deeper level. For one suspects that Le Corbusier's complicity with tourism may go far beyond stylistic references to cars, ocean liners and airplanes; rather it appears like an axiomatic theme in his life and work.

NOTE

This essay was read as a paper at the Institute of Fine Arts, New York University, New York on 24 January 2003. An earlier version was presented at the Le Corbusier symposium at the Architectural Association in London in March 2001. For a more complete discussion, including bibliographical references, see my 'Voyages en Zigzag', in S. von Moos and A. Rüegg (eds.), *Le Corbusier before Le Corbusier*, New Haven and London, 2002, pp. 23–43 and 283–5. It goes without saying that this essay is based on the research of many authors. Among them, I wish to single out H. Allen Brooks, Beatriz Colomina, Giuliano Gresleri and Mogens Krustrup, whose work and friendship have been particularly inspiring.

Contributors

Tim Benton is Professor of Art History at the Open University, where he has taught since 1970. His publications on Le Corbusier include *The Villas of Le Corbusier*, and a number of essays on individual houses in *Rassegna*, *Quaderns*, *AA Files*, *Ein Haus für den Kubismus* and volume seven of the Garland edition of the Le Corbusier Archive. He has also contributed to a number of major exhibitions including *Thirties: British Art and Design before the War*, *Le Corbusier Architect of the Century* and *Art and Power*. Most recently, he was consultant curator, with Charlotte Benton, of the *Art Deco* exhibition at the Victoria & Albert Museum.

Peter Carl began working on Le Corbusier at Princeton, graduating in 1968, MArch in 1972 (after a stint in the US Navy). In the US he worked with Kenneth Frampton, Antony Vidler, Emilio Ambasz and Michael Graves (the latter during the end of his 'cubist' period), and taught at the University of Kentucky. Since 1979 he has taught at the University of Cambridge, where he continues to teach Diploma design and the graduate programme in History and Philosophy of Architecture.

Hilde Heynen is Associate Professor in Architectural Theory at the Katholieke Universiteit Leuven, Belgium, and has taught courses at the AA Graduate School. She has contributed to a number of architectural periodicals including *Assemblage*, *Archis*, *Harvard Design Magazine* and *The Journal of Architecture*. Her books include *Architecture and Modernity: A Critique* (1999) and an anthology of major twentieth-century Dutch texts on architecture co-edited with André Loeckx, Lieven De Cauter and Karina Van Herck. She has also co-edited *Back from Utopia: The Challenge of the Modern Movement* (2002) with Hubert-Jan Henket.

Architectural writer and designer **Charles Jencks** is the author of, among many other titles, *Le Corbusier and the Tragic View of Architecture*, *The Language of Post-Modern Architecture*, *The Architecture of the Jumping Universe* and *Le Corbusier and the Continual Revolution in Architecture*.

Mohsen Mostafavi is Chairman of the AA School of Architecture, a position he has held since 1995. Prior to this, he taught at Harvard University, the University of Pennsylvania, Cambridge University and the Frankfurt Academy of Fine Arts (Staedelschule). His research has been published in many journals, and he is co-author of *Architecture and Continuity* (1983); *Delayed Space* (1994); and *On Weathering* (1993), which received the American Institute of Architects' commendation prize for writing on architectural theory. Recent publications include *Approximations* (AA/MIT, 2002) and *Surface Architecture* (with David Leatherbarrow; MIT, 2002).

Daniel Naegele is an architect and critic and teaches in the Department of Architecture at Iowa State University. A graduate of the AA and Yale University, he completed his dissertation, 'Le Corbusier's Seeing Things: Ambiguity and Illusion in the Representation of Modern Architecture', under the supervision of Joseph Rykwert at the University of Pennsylvania. His articles on Le Corbusier and on representation in modern architecture have appeared in numerous journals worldwide.

Fernando Pérez Oyarzun teaches at the Catholic University in Santiago, Chile and was Dean of the Faculty of Architecture and Fine Arts there from 1990 to 2000. He has been involved in research and teaching in both Europe and the US, at Harvard University, University of Cambridge and Terza Universita di Roma among others. His publications include *Le Corbusier y Sudamerica: Viajes y Proyectos*.

Stanislaus von Moos is Professor of Modern Art at the University of Zurich. He has written on Renaissance architecture, on Le Corbusier and on Venturi, Scott Brown & Associates as well as on the history of industrial design in Switzerland.